Robert Campbell

IMPLOSION: AN ANALYSIS OF THE GROWTH OF THE FEDERAL PUBLIC SERVICE IN CANADA (1945-1985)

D1228024

IMPLOSION: AN ANALYSIS OF THE GROWTH OF THE FEDERAL PUBLIC SERVICE IN CANADA (1945-1985)

NICOLE MORGAN

The Institute for Research on Public Policy/
L'Institut de recherches politiques

Copyright   The Institute for Research on Public Policy 1986
All rights reserved

Printed in Canada

Legal Deposit Second Quarter 1986
Bibliothèque nationale du Québec

Canadian Cataloguing in Publication Data

Morgan, Nicole S. (Nicole Schwartz), 1945-
Implosion: an analysis of the growth of the
federal public service in Canada (1945-1985)

Prefatory material in English and French.
Issued also in French under title: Implosion :
analyse de la croissance de la Fonction
publique fédérale canadienne, 1945-1985.
ISBN 0-88645-037-3

1. Civil rights--Canada. 2. Canada--
Officials and employees. 3. Canada--
Politics and government. I. Institute
for Research on Public Policy II. Title.

JL108.M6713 1986   354.71006   C86-090147-5

The Institute for Research on Public Policy
L'Institut de recherches politiques/
2149 Mackay Street, Suite 102
Montreal, Quebec H3G 2J2

CONTENTS

FOREWORD

For several years, there has been considerable debate regarding the nature, role and growth of the Canadian public service. Between 1910 and 1985, the number of federal public servants grew from 20,000 to approximately 225,000, almost one-third of whom are in the national capital area. In May 1985 the new federal Conservative Government announced that the number of federal employees would be cut by 15,000 over 5 years.

In this book, Nicole Morgan traces the growth and the development of the federal public service from the period following the Second World War to 1985. She suggests several hypotheses, including one regarding the role played by the federal public service in absorbing surplus labour on two occasions: after 1940 when returning veterans were hired under the veterans' preference clause; and after 1965, when the first cohorts of Canada's baby boom entered the labour force. The author, who was a public servant from 1981 to 1985, combines statistical data and in-depth interviews in her analysis.

The Institute believes it is both timely and important to publish this study. It should prove particularly useful to those interested in following developments in the public service, and will contribute to a better understanding of issues relating to government. This book follows a previous study on the public service by Nicole Morgan entitled Nowhere To Go? (Où Aller?), which was also published by the Institute. In view of the importance of the topic, the Institute is publishing Mrs. Morgan's latest book in French and English.

Rod Dobell
President

December 1985

AVANT-PROPOS

Il se fait, depuis quelques années, un débat très vif sur la nature, le rôle et la croissance de la Fonction publique au Canada. Entre 1910 et 1985, le nombre des employés fédéraux est passé de 20 000 à environ 225 000, dont le tiers est en fonction dans la Région de la capitale nationale. En mai 1985, le nouveau gouvernement conservateur à Ottawa annonçait son intention de procéder à des coupures de 15 000 employés échelonnées sur une période de cinq ans.

Dans son ouvrage, Nicole Morgan retrace la croissance et le développement de la Fonction publique fédérale de la fin de la Deuxième Guerre mondiale jusqu'en 1985. Elle propose un certain nombre d'hypothèses, l'une d'entre elles voulant que la Fonction publique ait joué un rôle clef pour éponger les surplus de main-d'oeuvre à deux moments de son histoire. D'abord après 1940, alors que ceux qui avaient combattu outre-mer furent embauchés en vertu de la clause dite de priorité consentie aux anciens combattants. Puis après 1965, alors que les premières cohortes du <u>baby boom</u> firent irruption sur le marché du travail. L'auteur, qui fut attachée à la Fonction publique de 1981 à 1985, appuie son analyse sur des données statistiques et des interviews.

L'Institut est d'avis qu'il est opportun et important de publier cette étude. Elle devrait se montrer particulièrement utile à ceux qui s'intéressent à la vie de l'administration publique et contribuer à une meilleure compréhension des problèmes de gouvernement. Cet ouvrage fait suite à une autre étude de Madame Morgan sur la Fonction publique, intitulée <u>Où Aller?</u> et publiée elle aussi par l'Institut. Vu l'importance du sujet, l'Institut a cru bon de publier ce dernier texte en anglais et en français.

Rod Dobell
Président

Décembre 1985

THE AUTHOR

Nicole Morgan was born in France in 1945. There she studied philosophy and the social sciences. After teaching philosophy she developed a specialization in prospective analysis and planning at Futuribles in Paris. She has acted as a consultant for numerous companies, including IBM, Renault, and Kodak-Pathé.

Mrs. Morgan became a Canadian citizen in 1976. She has more recently become especially interested in human resources planning and has published several articles on the possible disappearance of mandatory retirement. She is also the author of a study on public service management, published by the Institute for Research on Public Policy under the title Nowhere to Go? in 1981. That same year she entered the federal public service, where she remained until 1985.

Mrs. Morgan lives in Ottawa with her husband and their two children.

ACKNOWLEDGEMENTS

I would like to thank the Institute for Research on Public Policy for allowing me such great freedom of expression and for publishing this work with such speed. My thanks to Dominique Clift for the profound attention he devoted to editing my text.

I would also like to express my thanks to the Public Service Commission which graciously made data available to me; I appreciate this all the more since the data were as yet unpublished.

Above all I would like to express my deepest gratitude to all the public servants toiling in the shadows who helped by providing me with their advice, information, criticism and their unfailing encouragement. . .which I sorely needed! Above all, my thanks to EX4 and Charles Moubarak.

Nicole Morgan

SUMMARY

Theme

The theme of this book is the apparently uncontrollable growth of bureaucracy and the budget deficit which the public tends to associate with it. The book's introduction reviews this criticism and several others levelled at public servants in general and federal ones in particular. The conclusion is that in spite of the social changes which have shaken this country since the Second World War and in spite of the fact that public employees at all levels of government now constitute a third of the Canadian labour force, the image of the mean and dishonest "servant" still persists in the minds of the public and politicians alike. This continually leads to highly emotional reactions, half sarcastic and half indignant, which have taken the place of any real knowledge. The management of the public service attracts even less attention on the part of the public than that of a hotel kitchen.

Argument

Housekeeping has never been exciting, elevating, or stimulating; nevertheless it is the basis of every human activity. Hence it has been the stumbling block of ideas, ideologies and cultures. The public service is, after all, housekeeping on a grand scale and, as such, deserves a closer examination than it has been receiving. In a sense, it is the magnifying mirror for the society at large. This book is therefore a call for a better understanding of the changes which have overtaken the public service since the end of the Second World War. It seeks to avoid the national pastime of bureaucracy-bashing, even though at times it is highly critical of the way the public service has been managed by the politicians and the bureaucrats themselves. Above all, the book seeks to bring a new perspective to our recent history.

Hypotheses

Five hypotheses are put forward. They are clearly hypotheses and presented as such because the lack of reliable data precludes the kind of foolproof demonstration that social scientists are always so keen to offer.

The first hypothesis states that there was an unconscious motive behind the growth of the public service. It consisted in mopping up the labour surpluses which arose on two occasions:

- after 1940, when returning war veterans were hired under the veterans' preference clause, thereby causing the public service to come close to tripling over a period of twelve years;
- after 1965, when the first waves of the enormous Canadian baby boom hit the labour market, thereby causing the public service to double over a period of ten years.

The federal service absorbed more than its share of these two groups, with the result that during the 1950s its average age was higher than that of the Canadian labour force, and during the 1970s it was lower.

One could say that the public service took over a role that historically had been played by the church and the army. While there is no question of limiting the functions of the church, the army and big government to this sole dimension, one should not underestimate society's unconscious need to keep most of its members occupied in one way or another.

The second hypothesis states that the size of the expansion is not as important as the mentality of the people who are part of it. The first period of growth was unparalleled but had no effect on the traditional structure of the public service. In this instance, growth was carefully managed; it was concentrated in a few departments, distributed fairly evenly across the country, and made up of older men whose outlook had been shaped by the Hungry Thirties and the war. In a period of intensive growth, the civil service as it was then called was modelled on our military. This influence lingered on in some departments and central agencies well into the seventies. Although the second period of growth was less important in terms of numbers, it revolutionized both the structure and role of the public service. This expansion was based on young university graduates, mostly in economics, business administration and the social sciences. These people were eager to respond to the new demands formulated by an extraordinarily young country. At that time, one Canadian out of two was under thirty.

The third hypothesis states that, in the rush, everyone neglected the idea of management, assuming quite wrongly that productivity, motivation and accountability in government were the same as in private enterprise. This led to six serious structural imbalances which eventually overwhelmed and crippled public service managers:

- Imbalance in the career pyramid with 55 per cent of male civil servants in Ottawa-Hull being at middle management level. In some departments, the imbalance is such that senior levels are more numerous than subordinate ones.
- Imbalance in the treatment of women who did not benefit from either wave of expansion. In Ottawa-Hull in 1984, women represented 44.5 per cent of the public service but only 16.2 per cent of management personnel.
- Imbalance in the structure of the public service with a disproportionate number of staff personnel as opposed to line.
- Imbalance in the age pyramid as a stagnant public service had closed its doors to the younger generations, particularly young men, thereby repeating earlier mistakes in human resources planning.
- Imbalance in time management as public servants became excessively mobile during the seventies and part of the eighties.

In the seventies alone, over one million staffing actions were filed, leaving little time for experience and actual management of government programs.

- Psychological imbalance as the motivation of public servants was completely ignored and as the evaluation and merit systems collapsed under the pressures generated by feverish growth.

The fourth hypothesis states that the next ten years will bring about a growing awareness that the public service cannot possibly keep on growing endlessly, and that its resources are limited. There will be years of considerable confusion since that institution was organized at the turn of the century and has, with a few exceptions, not stopped growing. The outlook will seem particularly depressing and confusing because during the giddy years of expansion, the code of ethics, the evaluation and merit systems were allowed to break down to the point where they will have to be reconstructed from scratch. The public service will not only have to deal with the crucial internal problem of motivation at a time when growth has come to a halt and when the mistakes of the past must be repaired, it will also have to reconsider its relationship with its political masters and with all Canadians. It will have to face the dilemma of deciding if it should become representative of the Canadian mosaic and how to implement this in a period of zero growth. The only thing that might save the institution from outright revolt is the age factor: people in the public service, as they grow older, will tend to meet frustrations with resignation. On the other hand, superannuation and job engineering can be expected to be key issues at the end of the eighties.

The fifth hypothesis is still embryonic but could lead to a new kind of reflection on the ultimate fate of the public service and of "governability." It is possible that modern societies will evolve towards a kind of public service which is less and less monopolistic and which competes with the private sector on certain kinds of services. The possibility is not so much that of the private sector becoming more public, but of the public sector becoming more like the private one.

Method

The method is that of an historical analysis unfolding like a narrative.

For each time period studied, the public service—particularly the bureaucracy located in Ottawa-Hull—is examined in its socio-economic context, with the analysis focusing on internal changes in composition, organization and mentality.

This study has relied on unpublished data especially formulated for it by the Public Service Commission, as well as on open-ended interviews with some fifty public servants of all levels and ages.

There is little attempt to examine exhaustively the questions of language and of women's representation. This is not due to a lack of sensitivity but of time: the problem of representation in the public service requires a study of its own.

Style

Because the study mixes data, interviews and social analysis, the style is more lively than that of formal textbooks on this matter. It was a conscious decision on the part of the author to tell the story in this manner: it is clear that the ignorance surrounding the federal public service is largely due to the obscurity of the vocabulary with which it is discussed and which at times seems borrowed from that of medieval monks.

ABRÉGÉ

Le thème

L'ouvrage porte sur la croissance bureaucratique en apparence incontrôlable et sur le déficit budgétaire que le public tend à lui attribuer. L'introduction examine cette accusation et plusieurs autres qui visent les fonctionnaires en général et ceux du gouvernement fédéral en particulier. Car malgré les changements sociaux qui ont secoué le pays depuis la Deuxième Guerre mondiale et malgré le fait que l'administration publique occupe plus du tiers de la population active au Canada, l'image du serviteur vil et malhonnête est encore ancrée dans l'esprit du grand public et des hommes politiques. Elle ne cesse de provoquer des réactions émotives qui chevauchent le sarcasme et l'indignation, et qui prennent la place d'une connaissance réelle. On s'intéresse encore moins à la gestion de la Fonction publique qu'à l'intendance d'une cuisine d'hôtel.

L'argument

Et pourtant, même si l'intendance paraît la manière la plus fastidieuse et la plus vulgaire d'utiliser son esprit, elle est à la base de toute entreprise; elle est la pierre d'achoppement des idées, des idéologies et des cultures. En ce sens, l'on cherche à démontrer que les Fonctions publiques, qui sont après tout de l'intendance à grande échelle, sont les

xxi

mirroirs grossissants de la société et méritent, de ce fait, que l'on y regarde de plus près. Ce livre est donc un appel à la meilleure compréhension de ce qui s'est passé dans la Fonction publique depuis la Deuxième Guerre mondiale, une compréhension qui, espérons-le, évitera de donner dans le sport national qui consiste à tirer sur les fonctionnaires; et ce même si, par moments, il critique la manière dont la Fonction publique fédérale fut gérée pendant des années par les bureaucrates de concert avec les hommes politiques. Ce livre veut, avant tout, prendre une certaine distance par rapport à notre histoire.

Les hypothèses

Le livre repose sur cinq hypothèses qui resteront des hypothèses dans la mesure où le manque de données fiables rend quelquefois difficile ce genre de démonstration éblouissante et définitive qui est le rêve de tout analyste en sciences humaines.

Selon la première hypothèse, la Fonction publique fédérale eut pour but inconscient, à deux reprises, d'absorber un surplus de main-d'oeuvre :

- à partir de 1940, lorsque les anciens combattants de retour au pays furent embauchés prioritairement. La Fonction publique fédérale ne fut pas loin de tripler en douze ans.
- à partir de 1965, lorsque les premières cohortes de l'énorme baby boom canadien déferlèrent sur le marché du travail. La Fonction publique doubla en dix années.

Dans les deux cas, elle prit plus que sa quote-part du surplus : elle fut plus âgée que la population active pendant les années cinquante et elle fut plus jeune pendant les années soixante-dix.

On peut aller jusqu'à dire qu'elle assuma le rôle joué autrefois par l'Église et l'armée. Il ne s'agit pas bien sûr de réduire Église, armée et gouvernement à ce seul rôle, ce qui serait absurde, mais néanmoins de faire valoir que, dans l'inconscient collectif, l'on ne saurait sous-estimer la nécessité pour toute société d'occuper ses membres d'une manière ou d'une autre.

Selon la deuxième hypothèse, l'ampleur de la croissance joue un rôle secondaire comparativement à la mentalité des recrues. La première croissance de la Fonction publique fédérale fut unique par son amplitude mais elle n'altéra point sa structure traditionnelle. Ce fut une croissance prudemment gérée, limitée à quelques ministères, répartie dans les diverses régions du pays et composée d'hommes mûrs dont les mentalités avaient été forgées par les années de dépression et par la guerre. En ce sens, malgré une croissance rapide, le Service civil, tel qu'il s'appelait alors, se calqua sur le service militaire. Certains ministères et agences centrales en subirent l'influence jusque dans les années soixante-dix. À l'encontre de cette première croissance, la seconde, moins importante en nombre, révolutionna les structures et les rôles, composée qu'elle était de jeunes diplômés des sciences administratives, sociales et économiques, qui répondirent avec enthousiasme aux demandes d'un Canada extraordinairement jeune—un Canadien sur deux avait alors moins de trente ans.

Selon la troisième hypothèse, on oublia, dans la foulée, de gérer la croissance. L'on s'en tint à l'idée fausse que la productivité, les motivations et l'imputabilité du secteur public étaient identiques à celles du privé. Il en résulta toute une série de déséquilibres structurels devant lesquels les gestionnaires de la Fonction publique d'aujourd'hui se trouvent à la fois pantois et dépassés. Ces déséquilibres sont au nombre de six :

- déséquilibre de la pyramide des carrières alors que 55 pour cent de la population masculine d'Ottawa-Hull se retrouve au niveau cadre moyen ou supérieur. Dans certains cas le déséquilibre va jusqu'au renversement de la pyramide hiérarchique alors que les employés des niveaux supérieurs sont plus nombreux que ceux des niveaux inférieurs.
- déséquilibre entre les hommes et les femmes, ces dernières n'ayant pas profité des deux vagues de croissance. Elles ne représentent en 1984 que 16,2 pour cent des cadres mais 44,5 pour cent des fonctionnaires.
- déséquilibre entre les opérationnels et les fonctionnels.
- déséquilibre de la pyramide d'âge dans la mesure où la Fonction publique a fermé ses portes à la jeune génération, répétant ainsi les erreurs du passé en ce qui a trait à la planification des ressources humaines.

- déséquilibre temporel alors que, des années soixante-dix jusqu'en ce milieu des années quatre-vingt, la Fonction publique fut constamment agitée par des mouvements de troupes. Pendant les seules années soixante-dix, en effectuant plus d'un million d'actions de dotation faisant ainsi peu de place à l'accumulation de l'expérience et à la gestion même des programmes.
- déséquilibre psychologique alors qu'on ne fit aucun cas de la motivation des fonctionnaires et alors que le système d'évaluation et le principe du mérite s'effondrèrent durant la crise de croissance aiguë.

Selon la quatrième hypothèse, on devra prendre conscience, au cours des dix prochaines années, de ce que la Fonction publique ne va plus croître et que ses ressources sont limitées. Ce seront des années de confusion due en partie au fait que la grande organisation n'a connu que la croissance depuis le commencement de ce siècle sauf pour de brèves interruptions. Ce sera une période d'autant confuse et déprimante qu'au cours des années folles de la croissance on aura permis l'érosion de la déontologie, des systèmes d'évaluation et des principes du mérite, au point où l'on devra pratiquement repartir à zéro. Car il ne s'agira pas seulement de trouver le moyen de motiver les troupes dans une organisation stagnante mais aussi de reconsidérer sa situation par rapport au monde politique et au grand public. Il faudra également arriver à une meilleure représentation de la mosaïque canadienne et l'inscrire dans une organisation qui ne croît plus. . . et ne croit plus.

En fait, le seul facteur qui permettra de sauver la grande organisation d'une vague de révolte sera, une fois encore, l'âge de ses troupes. La Fonction publique va désormais vieillir rapidement et acceptera sans doute plus facilement les frustrations. Pendant ce temps, les problèmes de la retraite et de la flexibilité du travail deviendront des préoccupations primordiales.

La cinquième hypothèse est encore embryonnaire et elle concerne l'avenir à long terme de la Fonction publique et le problème de la "gouvernabilité". Il est permis de penser que les sociétés modernes s'en vont vers des Fonctions publiques qui se départiront peu à peu de leurs monopoles et se soumettront à la concurrence directe du secteur privé. Il est possible que ce ne soit pas le secteur privé qui évolue vers la fonctionnarisation mais plutôt l'inverse.

La méthode

La méthode utilisée est celle du simple récit historique qui fait état d'une partie de l'histoire de la Fonction publique à partir de la fin de la Deuxième Guerre mondiale jusqu'en 1985.

À chaque étape, l'on a tenté de replacer la Fonction publique, et plus particulièrement les effectifs de la capitale nationale, dans leur contexte socio-économique. L'on a voulu analyser en conséquence les changements démographiques, structurels et de mentalités qui se sont produits à l'intérieur du service.

La recherche s'est effectuée à partir de livres et d'articles, bien sûr; mais elle s'appuie également sur des données inédites fournies par la Commission de la Fonction publique et sur des interviews avec une cinquantaine de fonctionnaires de tous les âges et de tous les niveaux.

Si la recherche ne s'attarde pas sur les problèmes spécifiques des francophones et des femmes dans la Fonction publique, ce n'est pas par manque d'intérêt mais par manque de temps. La question de la représentation de la mosaïque canadienne mérite un ouvrage à elle seule.

Le style

Une dernière remarque sur le style. Parce que le livre est fait d'un mélange de données, d'interviews et d'analyse sociale, il veut être plus vivant que les ouvrages classiques en la matière. Mais il s'agit surtout d'une décision consciente de l'auteur de raconter une histoire de manière aussi animée que possible, supposant qu'une partie de l'ignorance qui entoure l'administration publique est due à l'utilisation d'un vocabulaire qui n'a parfois rien à envier au latin utilisé par les théologiens du Moyen Âge.

INTRODUCTION : 1984

Between 1910 and 1984, Canada's population tripled. Yet during the same period, federal public servants seemed to increase like fruit flies: their number went from 20,000 to a quarter of a million.

Such growth was neither continuous nor gradual. It was difficult to trace because the very definition of a government employee underwent numerous transformations throughout the years.[1] Sometimes the reasons had to do with statistics. At other times, they were influenced by politics. One example is Canada Post, which became a Crown corporation in 1981, thereby removing its employees from the scope of the federal public service.[2]

There were periods of stability. Between 1933 and 1936, for example, the number of federal employees remained at 40,000. A certain degree of uncertainty can be detected around 1923. There was also a period of feverish growth after World War II as the federal public service multiplied two and a half times, going from 49,739 to 131,646 between 1940 and 1952. This was the most dramatic expansion up to that time, but the one that is least discussed. The public service again doubled between 1965 and 1975 when it integrated the baby boom generation, or rather, when it was taken over by that generation.

As in most cases of weight gain, expansion was not evenly distributed. It was concentrated in the tertiary or administrative

1

sector of the bureaucracy which grew tenfold between 1965 and 1975 in the national capital. It was a living illustration of Parkinson's Law. By 1985 the so-called "Me Generation" had become middle-aged and the age pyramid of male employees in Ottawa-Hull began to show an inevitable bulge around the middle: more than 55 per cent were in management jobs and a third of them in middle management.

These figures represent only the tip of the bureaucratic iceberg. They do not include the public service of the provincial governments, which outgrew their federal counterpart,[3] or employees of municipalities, the parapublic sector, private companies subsisting on public funds, or such bureaucratic fallout as consultants, office cleaning and plant watering services, printers and dealers in office supplies and furniture.

According to current estimates, some 3.1 million Canadians are employed directly or indirectly by the State. This amounts to about 30 per cent of the labour force. With its 225,000 permanent employees, the federal service hardly stands out, numerically speaking. The major areas of expansion between 1961 and 1975 were in education and health care.

It must be stressed that this expansion did not always provoke the horrified outcries that one finds in the media today. There is a tendency to forget that up to the early 1970s the growth of the public sector was just one aspect of a broader trend, that it was perceived at that time as an investment in a prosperous future, and that this phenomenon was common to all industrialized societies.

Canadians then had very high expectations from a government which was eminently lavish with its largesse. It's true that the public debt swelled from $12 billion in 1960 to almost $17 billion in 1970 without unduly alarming the population which, in any case, was heavily committed to consumer credit. The word was that repayment could always be postponed to some later date. This attitude was totally in keeping with the extremely young population: in 1970 one Canadian out of two was under thirty.

To all those who like second-guessing the past and who wonder why the voice of wisdom was never heard denouncing the surge of

2

growth of the public service, public expenditures and budget deficits which are now seen as unhealthy, one could reply that such a voice would have been drowned out in the general euphoria of those days. When the future seems to beckon and smile, no self-respecting politician and no bureaucrat eager for promotion would dare forecast rainy days and urge drastic cutbacks. There were indeed a few mandarins of the old school of thought who worried at this turn of events, but nobody listened.

And yet it wasn't for lack of omens. At the beginning of the 1970s it was already clear that government machinery was creaking, prompting the then Auditor General, James Macdonnell, to utter his now famous phrase: "The Government has lost, or is close to losing, effective control of the public purse."[4] In great haste, a few hundred employees who had nothing whatsoever to do with the problem were laid off. But this was just a summer shower and optimism quickly returned.

It was short lived. The energy crisis, inflation, rising unemployment and soaring interest rates pulled Canadians out of their daydreams. Public debt had risen beyond reasonable levels, to the point that out of every three dollars spent by the government one was directed towards servicing it. Confidence turned sour. As Lance Liebman said," We have moved from our traditional self-assurance: 'we have done so much, we can do everything, and that's what we shall do to the pessimistic ideas that "nothing works", that large organizations only serve their own interests.' "[5]

Canadians were on the lookout for some shadowy culprits, scapegoats to whom they could point, apart from the obvious figures of the Prime Minister and his cabinet. The bureaucracy was set in the pillory and accusations were hurled in newspaper articles, editorials, and after-dinner conversations in every province.

"Whatever the beef," one senior official sighed," high food prices, postal strikes, high taxes, language policy, gun control, unemployment, abolition of capital punishment, the relaxation of abortion laws—Canadians seem(ed) to be developing a remarkable capacity for transforming that beef into chippy remarks about public servants. The

3

stage (had) not yet been reached where civil servants, like the official hangmen of yore, need to wear hoods when they do their work in public but they do feel increasingly obliged to apologize for their participation in the giant conspiracy of government to abuse the poor honest citizen, as perceived by that citizen."[6]

The phenomenon was almost universal, affecting wealthy societies from Great Britain to Australia and including the United States.[7] It wasn't even an original development; the first complaints of that nature go back to the Roman poet Juvenal, and since that time they have been subject to cyclical fluctuations the secret of which still remains to be explained. Drawing up an inventory of the complaints voiced against public servants in the course of history would no doubt keep dozens of scholars busy for a decade, with several years devoted to the heated relations between Canadians and their own "servants."

Canadian history is replete with attacks on the public service. They antedate Confederation and have been taken up with zest by successive generations. However, the last five years have shown an unprecedented level of bitterness with criticism being concentrated on three distinct fronts: economic, political and psychological.

The explanation might possibly be that, subconsciously and collectively, government employees are still perceived as wily servants, indentured, as it were, to each citizen, and the only category of people who can be loudly and publicly insulted. It is the last luxury the middle class can afford and the ultimate revenge of those who have little else to their name. These attitudes have deep emotional roots, they defy rational analysis and thrive on the widespread ignorance which surrounds public administration.

In a sense, it is worse than ignorance. It is an indifference operating at various levels, interdependent and mutually supportive.

Indifference is, first of all, political. Ministers and members of Parliament show little or no interest in the way the federal public service is run. One obvious reason is the lack of time, "the scarcest resource in Ottawa."[8] While it is true that at the turn of the century ministers were generally well-read in the classics, that they were acquainted with each and every one of their employees, and that the

4

Prime Minister could take on the additional responsibilities of Justice and Finance, this is no longer possible today, even if a minister continues to bear a theoretical responsibility for everything that goes wrong in his department, from the executive assistant who forgets a document on a table, to the clerk who has disposed of confidential papers without having them shredded, to the secretary who has placed the wrong letters in the wrong envelopes. In fact, even the most obtuse critics know that a minister can't possibly be in control of everything that takes place either at headquarters or in far-flung regional offices. It's not a question of recalling the names and the faces of thousands of employees. Nor is it a question of being on top of the countless administrative details for which he is ultimately responsible. No one is held to impossible tasks.

It must also be said that efficient administration doesn't provide the minister with anything other than the solitary satisfaction of duty well done. As far as the public is concerned, it is programs and tangible results that matter. "There are no votes in good management. Five ministers told me that," a top official in a Canadian province told the Auditor General.[9] And he added, "This phenomenon is not limited to Canada. A United States Cabinet Secretary, responsible for administering a department of 120,000 people, said during an interview: 'You learn very quickly that you do not go down in history as a good or bad Secretary in terms of how well you run the place—whether you are a good administrator or not. As a result, a Secretary often tends to ignore administrative things because it is not worth his time; it is not where he should put his emphasis.' "[10]

According to Kenneth Kernaghan the same kind of indifference prevails in the universities where public administration is perceived as a poor relation of political science. "This is not an original observation, but it is a good one," he says.[11]

Indifference is also shared by the general public which, in spite of its readiness to criticize, actually knows very little about the quarter of a million federal employees. A poll in Toronto shows that more than half the persons interviewed could only come up with Canada Post when asked to name a federal agency. A quarter of the respondents were unable to say what the public service did and many of them burst out laughing and said it didn't do anything at all.

As for the federal bureaucracy, it isn't contributing anything towards a solution to the problem, since it is incapable of self-examination. This enormous white elephant has no central controlling brain. It is like the diplodocus: because of its size, it needs a small series of brains at intervals along its spine. Three agencies are responsible for its administration: the Privy Council Office, the Treasury Board and the Public Service Commission. As in any triumvirate worthy of the name, they are more or less always in conflict. In fact, "the 1979 reports of both the Royal Commission on Financial Management and Accountability (Lambert) and the Special Committee on the Review of Personnel Management and the Merit Principle (D'Avignon) strongly emphasized the need for personnel management to operate under a single roof."[12] But nothing has ever been done, and the data originating from these three agencies are fragmentary and sometimes contradictory. The presentation of statistical data only adds to the confusion: they follow no set pattern, are obscure and so general that the most persistent journalist can only give up in despair and make do with comprehensive figures which are even more thoroughly misleading. But neither is this new: "Almost two decades ago, the Glassco Report complained that the data available on public sector employment in Canada were confusing and inconsistent. . . . Matters have not changed for the better since then, as any regular newspaper reader may have noticed."[13]

Finally, the law of silence weighs heavily on Ottawa. It is not that the city is deathly still; on the contrary, conversation is lively in a town where winters last for six months and individuals readily come together over a hot cup of coffee. However, since this is a small town, no one is allowed to stand out by talking openly to the press, for instance. Anyone foolhardy enough to do so would immediately be ostracized along with his family, and would encounter serious difficulties in finding another employer.

"No one in Ottawa," Sandra Gwyn relates in one of her articles, "has ever shoved a marked Globe and Mail under my door, or suggested I meet them in the bowels of the National Arts Centre's parking garage at four a.m. Make no mistake, though, Ottawa is a city full of "Deep Throats." To stalk the bureaucracy, as I have been doing these last several months, is to step inside the world of Woodward-Bernstein, bureaucratic horror stories have become almost a drug on the market. But finding officials, or former officials prepared to put their names to their out-of-office tales of woe is quite another matter."[14]

To discover what is going on inside that bureaucratic world, one ends up relying on wild stories spread by word-of-mouth, on rumour and gossip, and on impressions which try to focus on some kind of scapegoat or other within the bureaucracy itself (minorities, for example). The most virulent criticism of the bureaucratic world that one can hear in Ottawa comes from the bureaucrats themselves ... but always in private. There are things that have to be kept in the family. And feelings and impressions that are spread by rumour and gossip keep on proliferating because the authorities are saying nothing to their own employees that might help confirm or deny any criticism. The principal victims of this silence are public servants themselves.

Such remoteness and ignorance may appear perfectly justified. According to one perspective, government employees are, by definition, parasites, ill-adjusted and boring. The present consensus seems to be that the future of Canada will be played out in the private sector according to the country's ability to meet international competition.

The argument is not unfounded but it would be dangerous to accept it uncritically, given the numerical importance of the Canadian bureaucracy. Making up one third of the labour force, it is the most powerful pressure group in the country. It administers trillions of dollars and plays the role of social banker by redistributing tax revenues on the basis of criteria which it helps to define. Moreover, one should not forget that these three million people are taxpayers like the rest of us and are just as concerned about the future of the country as anyone else.

This infrastructure can't be compared to the shadowy power held by the 350 individuals who laboured with their wooden writing cases in pre-Confederation days.[15] The bureaucracy has become a social force in contemporary Canada. Its justification, its stewardship, its management, the integrity and the morale of its members, all of these have made it an integral part of the country's social and economic fabric which no longer justifies the wild or radical approach that says, "Kill them all, God will know his own."

We should remain optimistic. We will have to learn how to re-evaluate bureaucracy without any tinge of racism (is there another word for it?). There are many signs at present which suggest that the country is ready to have a close look at the future of government services. Concern is concentrated on five main issues.

I Limits of Public Sector Growth

Is expansion of the public service a necessary and unavoidable consequence of the modern state? Is it circumstantial and attributable to the necessity, for instance, of absorbing surplus manpower? Or are we moving towards some kind of amalgamation of the public and private sectors, in which government intervention would only be a question of degree? Would we find ourselves with agencies ranging from those that are exclusively governmental (ministries) to a majority of organizations with economic intervention such as that experienced by Crown corporations? Or are we moving in a totally opposite direction where government services would no longer be monoplistic in nature and would have to compete with the private sales and service sector?

II Cutbacks

Should we and can we reduce the public service at the federal, provincial and municipal levels? If so,

o   how do we eliminate government programs and fire the employees administering them?

o   do we keep as many programs as possible by resorting to automation and laying off the least productive employees?

o   should layoffs resulting from program shut-down be final or should employees be posted elsewhere in the public service? Is attrition a possible solution?

8

o   What would be the impact of massive and permanent public
service layoffs? What would the cost be in social and economic
terms? Would it be worth it?

III Productivity

What does the public service produce? Can it be compared to anything
in the private sector, or do we need another definition based on other
norms and standards? Which ones? Do public employees constitute a
special interest group like any other that seeks to protect its own
interests? Who is able to make a judgment on this? Can the
bureaucracy assess its own goals and performance?

IV Politics

To whom are public servants accountable? To the elected
representatives of the people, to Parliament, to Canadians? To
themselves inasmuch as they constitute a third of the labour force?
Where exactly is the dividing line between political and bureaucratic
power? Should public servants be politically neutral? Is Ottawa
gradually moving towards the American model? What will be the future
response to the thorny issue of political patronage in public
administration?

V Ethics

Should public servants have rights, responsibilites and a code of ethics
different from those of the population at large and thereby earn special
treatment? Should the public service become a social pace-setter and
be representative of the Canadian Mosaic? If so, what role should it
play in the political process: representative or advisory? What would
the public have to pay in exchange for representation? What would be
the terms of a contract that met the requirements of all parties?

The purpose of the present book is not to answer all of these
questions. The topic is too vast and it will be years before people are
able to deal with it in an objective and dispassionate manner. Its
purpose is more modest: to develop certain aspects of the first two

issues by analysing the growth of the Public Service of Canada since the end of World War II and concentrating on the region of the national capital (Ottawa-Hull).

The reason for this choice, apart from the obvious limitations of time and money, is that the growth of the public service in Ottawa and in Hull has, by exaggerating them, exacerbated all the tendencies exhibited by the larger bureaucracy. In this sense Ottawa is a striking caricature of what happened in Canada after the war in public administration and in private enterprise as well. This aspect of our social history acts as a magnifying mirror which few people care to look at because of the unflattering image they receive.

Starting from this microcosm we will put forward a series of hypotheses applicable to the growth of the public service in Canada which, in turn, will suggest a number of predictions.

The first hypothesis is that the public service has an unconscious role, namely to absorb surplus manpower. This function came to the fore on two separate occasions:

o   after 1940 as Canadian veterans returned home (the public service almost tripled in twelve years);

o   after 1965 when the first waves of the postwar baby boom hit the labour market (the federal public service doubled in ten years).

In a sense, the public service assumed a social function that had previously been performed by religious orders and the army. While it would be absurd to reduce public administration to this single dimension it would be equally so to reduce religious and military activity to purely practical solutions for a society which had no other answers for its surplus of young people. This integrating and socializing role is, nevertheless, far from being negligible in the light of those great unconscious historical motivations which are subsequently rationalized. Thus, wars are often explained with reference to Hegel's philosphy, but how many of them are really triggered by the need of elderly generals and statesmen to be rid of a large number of young people who are potentially dangerous to their power and who must be kept busy in some way or other?

The second hypothesis about the growth of the public service is

10

that numbers are not as important as the mentality of the newcomers. In this respect, the two periods of rapid expansion, one associated with the war, the other with the baby boom, each have distinctive features. In the first case, returning veterans were mostly mature men whose outlook had been shaped by depression and war. The quasi-military structure of the public service did not collapse under the strain. On the other hand, the expansion associated with the baby boom took place at higher levels in the hierarchy. They were university graduates whose mentality had been shaped by the social, economic and administrative sciences, as well as by their participation in a consumer society. Accordingly, the social and economic programs launched by the government during the 1960s and the 1970s were perhaps not so much a sign of a more compassionate society but rather a "new and improved product" which the young bureaucrats needed to bring onto the market in order to feel useful, to build their own empires, or both.

The third hypothesis is that the second wave of expansion produced a series of particularly unhealthy structural imbalances, especially in the national capital. The balance of power between Ottawa and the regions was broken as headquarters staff came to be over-represented. An acute hierarchical imbalance occurred in several departments due to a top-heavy authority structure and an overabundance of middle management. An administrative imbalance developed as the number of civil servants grew to be disproportionately large compared to the population served. There was an imbalance between the sexes as women who had been excluded from the two successive waves of expansion now faced the almost insurmountable prospect of seeking their share of a shrinking pie. And, finally, there was an age imbalance as the public service had closed its doors on the young generation.

According to the fourth hypothesis, the next ten years will be years of great confusion and despondency for the public service. It is in danger of deteriorating as the educational system did; a system whose development has already been stalled for some time by a generation of teachers who, during the period of rapid expansion lost the critical standards and motivations which once constituted important social

11

landmarks. In other words, personnel management in the public service finds itself in a kind of limbo deprived of the carrot of rapid turnover associated with periods of growth. It is mired in a system of classification and remuneration which inhibits responsibility. It is unable to put forward a system of penalties for poor performance thereby taking back the immunity which should never have been granted in the first place. In addition to being structural, the coming crisis will be a moral and ethical one. The public service lacks a philosophy of administration at the very moment that the private sector is engaged in formulating a new one. The public sector has fallen behind, yet this situation can eventually be corrected by borrowing some standards from the private sector; its norms obviously cannot be borrowed in their entirety. Public administrators must learn to think for themselves and to communicate their findings more effectively to their employees, to Canadians and their elected representatives. It will not be easy.

The following analysis will therefore develop these hypotheses by looking at the growth of the public service from three different angles:

o   the long-neglected demographic angle without which it is impossible to understand the 1960s and 1970s;

o   the structural angle, obscured by official statistics, by paying particular attention to changes in career patterns; and

o   the human angle, the one that causes so much anxiety, by probing the evolution of employee outlook.

This analysis will follow events in a chronological order, and will give an account of the growth experienced by this enormous organization from 1945 to the present day.

Note regarding Methodology

Even when such an analysis is reduced to three variables (demography, structure and psychology), it remains vast and complex. Just coming to terms with numbers is difficult enough because the demographic data put out by the Treasury Board and by the Public Service Commission are inconsistent. Moreover, the division between the public service proper which comes under the Public Service Employment Act and the whole public sector which includes Crown corporations and the armed forces resembles the fluctuating frontiers of medieval Europe. There are no data available which would make it possible to compare age of entry, promotion rates and mobility between one generation and another, or even within one generation. For Ottawa-Hull it was necessary, on occasion, to resort to government telephone directories as a substitute.

Structural analysis was even more difficult. Studies on the hierarchy are few and far between, and official data are presented under such irrelevant headings as occupational categories. Tasks are divided into six broad categories which for all these years have masked the true nature of the hierarchy of public servants and its changes. Specifically, they have hidden the extent of classification creep, the rise of the middle class, the much more serious disparities between men and women, as well as the real career structure in certain departments. In order to probe the structure, it was therefore necessary to make use of other variables in the Public Service Commission's computer database which go back only to the very recent past—1976.

Because of time limitations and the technical problems involved, the analysis of employee mentality has had to be limited to the perceptions of some fifty people expressed in open-ended interviews. The problem was not in finding people eager to talk about their jobs, but in not confining ourselves to those who feel profoundly frustrated by the current situation.

Obviously, there are many faults of omission. The specific and yet highly important issues of bilingualism and equal opportunity in the public service have barely been discussed. This is not due to a lack of awareness but lack of time and, above all, the author's wish to deal with these topics in greater detail in later articles and monographs.

1: FROM LOW PROFILES TO HIGH FLYERS

The War is Over

In 1940, Ottawa was a rather sleepy town of 250,000 people. One resident out of thirty was permanently employed by the federal public service: 7,507 persons, the majority of whom must have known each other at least by sight. There were also 6,513 persons on the fringes of the organization, temporarily employed in various tasks, mostly manual, ranging from typing for the ladies to freight handling for strong men. Unfortunately, no one ever took the trouble of describing their apparently lackluster existence. However, we do catch fleeting glimpses of it in the handwritten service memos which are filed away in the National Archives.

In 1945, at the end of World War II which had taken the lives of 44,000 Canadians, the number of permanent federal employees in the national capital dropped to 6,777, but the number of temporary employees had grown fivefold. There were 27,963 of them, the majority war veterans. The city became, in the words of R. MacGregor Dawson, "one great big blooming buzzing confusion."[1]

Indeed, this was the atmosphere throughout the whole country. For the first time, the Civil Service Commission was explicitly given the mandate for a primary social role: to provide work rapidly and at any cost for all those who were returning home from the war. At the outset of hostilities, it had been decided that temporary jobs would be opened up in the public service and that the veterans' preference clause of 1918 according job preference to veterans' for any public service job vacancy, would be re-activated.

This political gesture was not devoid of a Machiavellian touch. No government in the world can contemplate the return of a large mass of young men, many of whom have been trained in the consummate art of violence without a certain degree of apprehension . Already in 1917 Sir Robert Borden's ministers had openly declared their concern about the homecoming of "potential bolsheviks", as they put it. They pressed the civil service to absorb some of them. The veterans' preference clause was thus the hybrid product of patriotism and fear. Ambiguity produced hesitation, and the veterans' preference clause was applied rather sluggishly. It must be added that the civil service at the time numbered only about 10,000 employees, and it was very unlikely that its hiring policies would really be seen as an effective rampart against bolshevism.

Time went by, and the Russian Revolution gradually faded from memory. In 1940, as Parliament was debating the possibility of opening the federal civil service to war veterans, there was no one to bring out the red herring of revolution, even though there was no doubt that the idea had occurred to more than one of Mackenzie King's ministers.[2] This time, the bugbear was the Depression of the 1930s, and everyone was determined to prevent the recurrence of such a disaster, just as dangerous for society as revolution. Nonetheless, cabinet ministers were sincere in wanting to express their gratitude to those who had served their country so well.

The concept of merit was a weighty one for Canadians of that period who had demanded and obtained an end to the political patronage rampant in the civil service in favour of a more enlightened principle.[3] The struggle had been launched at the turn of the century.[4] It had come to a head on the return of World War I veterans when it became apparent that the jobs to which they had a rightful claim had gone to faithful supporters of the party in power. "Patronage was thus identified with those who grew rich at home while others suffered and died in France."[5] Canadians rose up in anger.

In fact, Canadians do not associate the word "merit" with "elitism," a concept which connotes privilege. It must be understood as applying to appointments made on any basis but that of political patronage which, as was demonstrated in 1984, is still repugnant to most people.[6] In this perspective, the qualifications of war veterans for office work hardly mattered: the important thing was that they were politically clean. The idea of merit as it applied to them was morally evident.[7]

It was a stormy debate. Its object was the preferential treatment accorded to disabled war veterans rather than the principle of affirmative action, a name which government policy in this respect never had.

It was not an idle debate. In the words of a former member of the Civil Service Commission, the task was "worthy of the labours of Hercules." More than a million men had gone abroad (1,081,865) seven-tenths of whom were expected back home. "In 1944, veterans were given an entire new department, to be directed by a full-fledged cabinet minister, the sole purpose of which was to look after the interests of veterans. Other relevant legislation included the Veterans Insurance Act, the War Services Grants Act, the Veterans Land Act, the War Veterans Allowance Act, and the Civilian War Pensions and Allowances Act—all passed in the period from 1944 to 1946."[8]

The Civil Service Commission, notorious for its lack of diligence, tackled the task with unusual efficiency. At the beginning of the war, it began planning for the eventual repatriation of military personnel. It opened recruitment centres in France, the Netherlands, Italy, and especially, as early as 1941, in Great Britain. This was necessary because the men began returning in massive numbers between 1940 and 1945, a period during which the public service expanded from 49,739 to 115,908 employees, both permanent and temporary.

It must be pointed out that although such growth was somewhat artificial, it cannot be explained solely on the basis of gratitude. The war effort had called for as many administrators, engineers, co-ordinators and clerical staff, as it had for military personnel. There is

17

a tendency to forget that wars are sustained and sometimes won by an administration which is invisible yet present in the daily life of front line troups. Therefore, a large proportion of the jobs offered to veterans were most likely needed for the war effort and would have been created anyway.

It must also be pointed out that the management of such a large number of employees required an extensive supporting staff of stenographers, typists, secretaries and telephone operators. By 1945, 21,000 women had joined the ranks of the bureaucracy, most of them on a temporary basis. And yet there were never enough. The annual reports of the Civil Service Commission complained repeatedly during the ten year postwar period how difficult it was to recruit and hold female support staff who, in good old military tradition, were referred to as "the girls."

Once the war was over, the flood of new personnel tapered off but did not dry up. By 1952 Canada had a civil service very much larger than its armed forces. Within twelve years, the number of federal employees had almost tripled. Out of 136,646 employees, one third were war veterans.[9]

The postwar growth of the federal public service was the most important one due to its scope. It was proportionately greater than the expansion of the 1960s and 1970s when the number of federal employees merely doubled. Yet it was a trouble-free expansion, a tidal wave without a storm. There were no doubt countless frustrations associated with the process. But it did little to change the routine and the mentality of the organization. . . at least for some time. Why?

First of all, the expansion was a prudent one. Obviously, there were massive hirings. But most of the people involved were hired on a temporary basis, following the oft-repeated motto of Henri Bland, former chairman of the Civil Service Commission, "Everything in its own time." It should be pointed out that the decision-makers of the postwar period were still under the shock of the war itself and of the Great Depression which had marked their childhood. Prime Minister Louis Saint-Laurent, in power since 1948, his ministers and advisers, as well as the chairman of the Civil Service Commission, firmly believed

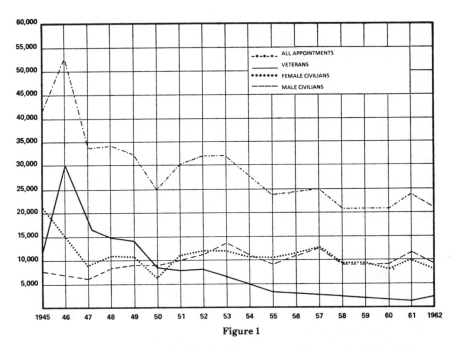

Figure 1

Appointments to the Civil Service, Permanent and Temporary, 1945 to 1962

Source: J.E. Hodgetts, William McCloskey, Reginald Whitaker and V.
           Seymour Wilson, The Biography of an Institution, The Civil
           Service Commission of Canada 1908-1967, The Institute of
           Public Administration of Canada, Montréal and London, McGill
           Queen's University Press, 1972.

19

that another depression was just around the corner and that the country would have problems making the transition from a war-time to a peace-time economy. Their pessimism was matched by that of economists who forecast a return to the conditions of 1939. At that time, industrial unemployment stood at 20 per cent and affected some 600,000 workers. There were also close to a million people on public relief and another 200,000 dependent on municipal relief. Accordingly, government policy was inspired more by fear of the past than by confidence in a promising future. Decisions were founded on the belief that the primary function of government was an economic one, with the idea of warding off the return of the Hungry Thirties. There was a general willingness to provide jobs for war veterans, but neither the public sector nor private enterprise was ready to promise them more than temporary employment.

The number of temporary employees quickly outstripped that of the permanent staff which remained fairly stable during the postwar years, remaining at about 30,000 and growing by only three per cent by 1950. In 1947, 76.2 per cent of federal employees had been hired on a temporary basis. This meant:

o   they could be fired by a simple administrative decision, while an order-in-council was required for the appointment and   dismissal (a very rare event) of any permanent employee;

o   temporary staff had to go through the regular procedure of contract renewal;

o   they were not eligible for all fringe benefits;[10]

This does not mean that there was no hope of joining the first class travellers, the group of permanent employees with their prized job security. But this hope did not exist in the form of a right and did not express itself as a claim or a demand. The Civil Service Commission, still all-powerful in this respect, was responsible for recruitment and appointments. It was careful not to hurry things along, as it was still recovering from the shock of having seen its whole staffing apparatus increase tenfold in five years. Between 1945 and 1954, it made more than 44,000 permanent appointments, which means that the number of candidates' files examined must have been one hundred times that number.

In 1946, the Commission began looking at individual transfers from temporary to permanent staff. But it drove a hard bargain, negotiating a lower job classification in exchange for job security. Some gratefully seized the proferred opportunity. As a former commissioner explained, "Acquiring permanent status was one of the important events in one's life. It was talked about months before and months after it took place. . . . People lived that whole period on the basis of events like that."

Those who had given in to their misgivings about the future, and had accepted a lower salary in exchange for job security, soon discovered that they had made a very poor bargain. By 1948, those who passed from temporary to permanent staff were no longer penalized. The economy, while still fragile, had not collapsed. New government programs needed a larger permanent staff and the percentage of temporary employees dropped from 76.2 to 59.4 by 1952. Between 1945 and 1954, the Commission appointed 44,602 permanent employees, more than half of whom were war veterans. In fact, two-thirds of all male appointments in the postwar period were made under the veterans' preference clause.[11]

Nevertheless, until the beginning of the 1960s, there were more temporary than permanent employees, which is an indirect indication that the majority of federal jobs were concentrated in the lower echelons of the public service. Permanence was still the exception that confirmed the rule.

Unlike the later wave of expansion associated with the baby boom, postwar growth did not affect the upper reaches of the hierarchy immediately, especially not the controlling agencies at the centre of government.

Postwar growth was localized. The departments of Defence, Veterans' Affairs and the Post Office absorbed over 60 per cent of the war veterans in government service. On the other hand, the expansion associated with the baby boom generation affected all of the public service except these three departments which were heavyweights in terms of numbers but lightweights in terms of political muscle. Postwar growth was particularly important outside the national capital.

The proportion of federal employees in other parts of the country rose from 59 per cent in 1945 to 75 per cent by 1952. During the 1970s however, when the baby boom generation invaded the public service, growth was concentrated mainly in the Ottawa-Hull district.

Until 1948, the expansion of public service employment took place mostly in the lower levels as clerical and manual workers were being hired. After 1948, training and educational programs for veterans began to bear fruit[12] and appointments began to take place at higher levels. Gradually the veterans began to penetrate the upper reaches of the bureaucracy and, according to certain reports, the central agencies. But this was on a relatively small scale.

A third difference between the two successive waves of expansion has to do with hiring age and mentality. The postwar wave was made up of people who were mature and whose average age was around thirty, while the wave of the 1960s involved people who were still relatively young. In 1954, when the veterans had pretty well been absorbed into the system, the annual report of the Civil Service Commission noted that 20 per cent of all nominations concerned men over 40 years old, and 10 per cent men over 50 fifty. In 1961, the public service had aged considerably: almost 40 per cent of all federal employees were over 45 years old, which is 6 percentage points higher than the representation of the same age group in the general work force at that time.

Such an anomaly had numerous consequences. Everyone was aware that hiring on such a massive scale would be followed by relatively rapid attrition of the ranks. No career plans were necessary for people who, after the war, knew they would be there for only a limited time and who were happy to find steady and guaranteed employment.

The mentality of this generation, which had known the Great Depression and war before entering the labour market, was very different from that of the children it would be rearing. Expectations and ambitions were modest, and the values attached to work were, as we shall see later, financially conservative.

Military life was the perfect apprenticeship for bureaucratic discipline which rests on a visible hierarchy, an uncritical submission to orders, and a system of rewards involving promotions with little regard for personal initiative. This nuance was expressed in the name of the public service at that time: a civil service which was merely the continuation of military service without the uniforms. The generation of veterans who invaded the public service during the 1940s had been trained to obey and were tailor-made for the bureaucratic routine that dated from before the war. The new recruits were not there to overturn tradition but to conserve it. . . and that they did.

These considerations help to explain why such a massive influx of new employees in such a short time did so little to upset existing structures or even change the number of government departments. Apart from Veterans' Affairs, Defence Production was the only new department added to the relatively short list of 88 councils, agencies and departments which existed in Ottawa in 1950 (compared to 186 in 1975).

As for the lines of authority, they remained virtually unchanged even though mentalities had already started to change in the early 1950s. The time had not yet come for revolution. Everyday life resumed in the provinces and in a national capital which seemed as sleepy as ever.

Ottawa-Hull 1950

In 1950, Ottawa-Hull had not yet grown to 300,000 people. Suburban developments such as Manor Park and Alta Vista rose on what was then the periphery of the downtown core which itself had hardly changed since the 1930s, except for the construction of temporary offices for the departments of Revenue, Customs and National Defence. Apart from these ugly wooden structures, government offices were lodged in imposing stone monuments within sight of Parliament Hill.

This physical proximity represented much more than a practical arrangement. It was symbolic of the solidarity which for a long time exerted considerable influence on the Canadian mentality: the solidarity of the mandarins.

How Green Was My Valley

With the passage of time which plays such tricks on memory, the government of 1950 seems remarkably simple and enviable by today's standards. According to one observer: "It was in the image of those who composed it. Decisions were easy because those who made them were gentlemen."

Decision Making

In 1950 Louis Saint-Laurent had been in power for two years and would stay in office for another seven. It was a stable government which appointed stable ministers.[13] They were all-powerful, masters of their own ship... or almost. More particularly, ministers in charge of "departments representing essentially clientele or constituency interests ("vertical" line departments) often managed them as private preserves, even from the Prime Minister."[14] This was not because the Prime Minister had a weak personality, far from it. This was the traditional way government decisions were made.

Under Mackenzie King, for example, cabinet meetings were brief and infrequent, with sketchy notes for information purposes. In most cases decisions were made on the word of the minister submitting a proposal. The cabinet's agenda was simple and drafted in such a way that a new item could be tacked on at the last minute. There were only two Cabinet Committees: the Treasury Board, whose creation legend has attributed to Sir John A. Macdonald's alcoholic vapours,[15] and Defence; (a third one, Grain, existed only for a short time). These committees met sporadically in rare cases when disagreement existed between departments. As for the Prime Minister's Office and the Privy Council Office, they hardly existed at all, operating merely as high-flying secretariats.[16] In 1940 they amounted to a dozen people in all.

According to observers at the time,[17] most decisions were left to interdepartmental committees made up of top level bureaucrats. In most cases, economic and social policies were drafted with the tacit approval of ministers whose preoccupations were largely electoral. "When I arrived in Ottawa at the beginning of 1942," Mitchell Sharp, former mandarin and minister relates, "I recall Dr. Mackintosh's account of how he had been instructed to prepare a statement for

Mr. King to use when announcing on the radio the overall price ceiling which came into effect towards the end of 1941. He showed his draft to the prime minister who, after reading the opening paragraphs, looked up and said: 'This is important, isn't it Dr. Mackintosh?' "[18]

As the war effort intensified, the decision-making process became more formal and complex. Louis Saint-Laurent had the outlook of a modern manager. He had a precise mind; like Pierre Elliott Trudeau he had a horror of disorder and carelessness. Like him also, he would call on his ministers who were divided over a particular issue to discuss the question, he would sum up the pros and the cons, and then state his own opinion. This was the result of a good education rather than any desire to interfere in departmental affairs. The only one department which felt his influence directly was Justice, for the good reason that he personally administered that portfolio, a tradition which says a great deal about the relative simplicity of affairs of state at that time.

While the form may have changed, the substance remained the same: "Cabinet Committees tended to remain ad hoc rather than systematized. . . and interdepartmental committees of officials continued to flourish. Proposals were made directly to Cabinet and documentation by present standards was brief."[19] One could even say, and this might come as a surprise to many students of the federal public service, that this period represents the zenith of the mandarins' influence on Cabinet. And yet until the end of the 1950s, it was the kind of influence that was better accepted at that time than it is now. Why?

Personalities

No matter how powerful they may have been, the mandarins of 1950 appear to have had little influence on the everyday life of Canadians in general and on corporations in particular. The main reason is obvious. They were discreet to the point of invisibility. A glance at the Ottawa press during that period is particularly revealing in this respect. The names of top civil servants are rarely mentioned, and if so, it was usually to record a promotion, an honour granted, or a retirement, very much in the style of the paid advertisements published nowadays by private companies.

What people are prone to recall now, however, is neither the simplicity of government nor its discretion, but its personalized character. The public seems to have accepted the power of the mandarins because it had confidence in the ability of the decision-makers who, in turn, consistently showed themselves worthy of it. J.L. Granatstein has written an excellent book, The Ottawa Men,[20] full of admiration and respect for those who ran the federal public service between 1935 and 1957. His views are shared by many. To this very day, the incomparable talent of R.B. Bryce is the subject of stories like those that circulate about the exploits of famous generals. "There were dozens of stories told about how Bryce had drafted budgets that were models of ingenuity almost single-handed, how Bryce had conducted difficult fiscal negotiations with only the notes that would fit into his back pocket, how Bryce had dug his heels in on this policy or that policy, always urging restraint, usually prevailing when the politicians were on a spending rampage, stepping in to save them from their follies and guide them past their fears."[21]

Nevertheless, without questioning the personal qualities of these mandarins, displayed on countless occasions, one could point out that their quiet strength was partly circumstantial. They had the cohesiveness of small groups whose power is greater when power is concentrated rather than diffuse. James Eayrs has estimated that between 1945 and 1950 influential mandarins in Ottawa numbered about a dozen.[22]

Their influence was also derived from their homogeneity. As J.L. Granatstein writes: "They were a collection of old friends and colleagues who looked, sounded and spoke alike."[23] This is not surprising. In The Vertical Mosaic John Porter showed that the mandarins of that period all had the same Anglo-Protestant origin, they belonged to the upper class, and they had been educated in the best Canadian, American and British universities.[24] "They were all generalists recruited in the public service because of their brains and their non-specialized approach rather than their skills in particular disciplines, " Granatstein comments.[25]

They controlled information which, like government involvement, was relatively scarce, and it was reinforced by the fact that they met socially, at home, among friends, or at the Five Lakes Fishing Club in the Gatineau Hills.[26] This social kinship went hand-in-hand with their close proximity at work; their departments were all located on Parliament Hill. The three most important government bodies of that time were next door to each other: Finance, External Affairs and the Bank of Canada. As one retired deputy minister recalls, "There was no need for Committees since everyone met for lunch at the Château Laurier. More matters were settled around roast beef and potatoes in those days than around the overcrowded tables of the board rooms of the eighties."

The mandarins had the advantage of being respected by a society whose culture was not given to protest or to challenging authority, whether political, academic, ecclesiastical or bureaucratic. And, above all, they had stability. During the 1950s and the early 1960s, there were few changes in the bureaucratic pyramid of power, even though, before becoming Prime Minister in 1957, John G. Diefenbaker had sworn there would be.[27]

This stability was only a reflection of the social conservatism of governments currently in power. It was due to the relative lack of competition. The power pyramid was of the "pointed" type: there were few people at the superior and intermediate levels. Promotions were so rare that there was nothing to fear from "young turks" or from rising stars. Moreover, the mandarins of the 1950s were, as economist Richard A. Easterlin points out,[28] a happy community in the sense that they belonged to an age group that was neither numerous nor hard pressed by competition.

This generation saw public service as a vocation rather than as a professional activity, an attitude which fits in with the temper of the times. During the war and in the period that followed, "fighting for one's country," "to sacrifice oneself for the common good," and "to devote one's self to medicine and to teaching" were compelling social watchwords. Contemporary values required that government employees truly be civil servants, according to David Golden, a former deputy minister of that period: "I came into their world in the early fifties.

27

There is the old-fashioned word 'calling'. There was something of a religion about it in the old bureaucracy."[29]   This religion required humility, discretion and parsimony. "Everyone tended to pinch pennies, personally and at work, in programs and staff, but it was not calculated or a fetish. Simply there was a tacit, broad agreement about purpose and duty and responsibility and leadership. . . . "[30] Another civil servant recalls that parsimony covered everything "from non-existant office redecoration (I never had mine done) to the use of public transportation,[31] including the knee-jerk reflex of cutting spending programs. The message was clear: a good deputy minister was an economical one. . . and that's how most Canadians were too."

But in this regard no deputy minister ever surpassed the government's most influential economist, Assistant-Secretary of the Treasury Board, W.C. Ronson, whose obsessive concern with saving money had become legendary.[32]   If one considers that at that time the Treasury Board had the last word on public service expenditures, it is easy to see the kind of influence Ronson wielded over the internal and external spending of the public service during his fourteen-year term.

The Troops

Whether or not the attitudes of the mandarins were derived from contemporary circumstances, they undeniably shaped the minds of the bureaucrats over whom they presided. Nevertheless, like the problem of the chicken and the egg, the subordinates had already been cut from the same cultural cloth as their superiors. It must therefore be pointed out to all those who think that all it takes is to put moral and intellectual clones of the old mandarins at the head of the service, that we are not dealing here with the culture of a few who might have been the first, causal and innovating models; we are dealing with the culture of an entire period which all Canadians and some 130,000 public servants shared. And the leaders followed. . . as they had learned to do in school and later in the army: in good order and discipline.

The whole structure was remarkably stable. As Table 1 shows, few people left the public service. People entered for keeps.

Table 1: Comparison of Separation Rates, 1952-1955

	1952 %	1953 %	1954 %	1955 %
Civil Service of Canada[a]	14.03	16.09	13.8	13.3
All of Canadian industry	87.0	84.0	78.0	46.0[b]
Finance, insurance and real estate	43.0	46.0	39.0	28.0[b]
United States Civil Service	27.3	26.4	27.9[c]	24.4

a. Rates for the Canadian Civil Service do not include seasonal employees, nor student summer employees.
b. Rates for first eight months only.
c. Classified and wage employees.

Source: Public Service Commission, Annual Report, 1955.

The pyramid was hierarchical and stratified, and it had a broad base. Unfortunately, there are no statistical data with which to determine the exact structure of the public service at that time. Nevertheless, from the first pay scales published by the Commission in 1961, one can infer that wage disparities between the upper and lower levels were very large and that the career pyramid was more slender than at the end of the 1970s.

Furthermore, an examination of government telephone directories for the 1950s confirms the extrapolations drawn from salary scales: there were relatively few directors general, directors and people in intermediate positions. The slender career pyramid was designed to preserve the unified command at the top, "thereby sustaining the doctrine of ministerial responsiblity."[33]

The existing pyramid, associated with a low turnover rate, limited advancement opportunities which were so rare as to be highly unusual and considered events of extraordinary importance. Rivalries at the top and middle management levels were minimal because of a lack of suitable candidates. However, they were fierce at the bottom of the ladder where the odds of ever gaining advancement by means of rare so-called examinations were practically nil because of the large mass of employees. The recruitment of war veterans created the most severe tensions at these lower levels and they were all the more severe for not being expressed openly. According to a former secretary, "Office rivalries were secretly poisoning many lives, but the last thing one could do was talk about it."

In March 1951, The Public Service Review expressed satisfaction that the number of service examinations for 1950 had been the highest ever. "It reached 2,537, double the figure for 1949. It is about eight times the average for the years between 1931 and 1939, and almost three times the number for 1928, a prewar record, when it was 865."[34] Such enthusiasm says a lot about the attitudes of that period: a rapid calculation shows that only two per cent of federal employees were promoted in 1950. In other words, a federal employee could expect only one promotion during his entire career; those who were hired relatively late in life, the veterans, were sure of leaving at the same level they had come in.

The public service structure was also highly compartmentalized. There was no mobility between departments, and passage from one to another was extremely rare, even rarer than promotions. All accounts are agreed on this point: from the deputy minister down to the office clerk, careers unfolded in one and only one department.

Obviously, such departmental stability created a strong esprit de corps, with all its attendant advantages and disadvantages.

The whole world of subordinate employees was simple and reassuring. Everyone knew the deputy minister, the directors and the section heads, and greeted them in the corridors; deputy ministers usually knew all their employees, at least by sight. Oldtimers still talk about the annual June picnic for employees and their families, one of the rare occasions where social barriers were somewhat relaxed. Others remember the care with which deputy ministers sometimes handled the personal problems of their subordinates. "This was the kind of relationship that people later came to spurn but which meant everything to us. . . . Now we are no longer treated as human beings. . . . Before, we were like a small family. . . . I stayed in the same office with the same people for ten years. That creates bonds.

30

We helped one another if necessary, we knew each other well, we were all happy, much happier," said a former secretary.

This kind of paternalistic management within a stable organization is interesting not only for its anecdotal value or for the nostalgia it brings out for times gone by. It is now being rediscovered by the West through the intermediary of Japanese management practices.[35]

But life in the small bureaucratic world of Ottawa also had its darker side. It could be stifling after the forty-five hours of work required every week.[36] The absence of interdepartmental mobility was a sure-fire recipe for grudges and depressions. In fact, the situation was particularly difficult for outsiders, such as the francophones who did not speak English very well, or the very few women who had managed to take a few steps up the ladder. As one secretary recalls: "There was one woman engineer in my group. What she had to put up with is not even conceivable. In ten years she had not been invited once for a cup of coffee. And she stayed with us ten years." The solidarity within each department which was so reassuring for those who participated in it, could be threatening for employees of other departments. According to a retired office worker: "we didn't talk to others", meaning people in other departments. "We hardly had any opportunity of meeting them; people did not go to restaurants as they do today. From eight to five we were among ourselves, and at noon we ate a sandwich at our desk." Co-operation was hard to come by.

The simplicity of the hierarchical structure was offset by the classification system which a former manager described as "nightmarish." By the mid sixties, there were still 700 different types of positions and 1700 grades, each described in considerable detail, which had accumulated in the course of the century like layers of sediment on the floor of the sea. Not only were the "contents" of most jobs stipulated, but even the department to which they were assigned. There was, for example, an assistant chief auditor for National Defence, a head clerk for Customs and Excise, and a field officer for Indian Affairs. "When the late C.D. Howe set about the transformation of his old wartime Department of Munitions and Supply, which had relied heavily on the temporary assistance of experts from industry, into the Department of Defence Production, he was determined to have his choice of professional staff such as engineers and economists," L.W. Barnes relates. "The existing pay scales for these classes in the service were generally unattractive to competent employees in private industry and there was no particular incentive for those already in the service to move to the new department. The result was the establishment of a new class called Defence Production Officers. Pay scales were about one grade higher than those applicable to comparable professional classes in the rest of the service. Howe got his engineers and economists and the classification system became that much more illogical."[37]

Yet there are some who regret this classification system which gave each employee a sense of individuality and of belonging. As one of them explained, "We weren't simply any old AS 2 or PM 3 like thousands of others. One could be the chemist at the Mint. There was only one in Ottawa, and that was me." In other words, the title had a territorial connotation. Any theory of personnel management was the enemy. There was stubborn resistance against any territorial encroachments: "The Chairman of the Public Service Commission said it all when he exclaimed that the 'use of the title personnel officer or training officer (at that time) would have been sufficient to have one tried for witchcraft! ' "[38]

For anecdotal purposes let us add that in 1918, an attempt had been made to remedy this situation. A team of American consultants was called in at great expense. Not only was it a flop but it also provoked one of the rare instances of spontaneous revolt among federal employees. The Commission received thousands of letters, each one more vehement than the last, some going so far as to denounce the German-sounding names of certain consultants. The project was immediately abandoned. In 1946, a Royal Commission on administrative classification, chaired by Walter Gordon, tried more modestly to unravel the whole complex situation. Its conclusions were received and. . . shelved.

In a way, one might say that while the sixties and seventies put all their energies into promoting mobility, the fifties invested heavily in the defence of their professional turf.

The position so vigorously defended was obtained after successfully completing an examination held under the sole responsibility of the Civil Service Commission. Each nomination, promotion, and transfer had to touch all the bases set up by a centralized administration which required scrupulous observance of the letter of the law and tolerated no deviation, at least in theory. A job opening was announced, and the candidates were registered and screened. The date of the examination was set and the employees gathered in a hall for a written test. The number of candidates sometimes reached levels that are hard to imagine today. Annual reports of the forties note national examinations where the number of competitors reached several thousands. The record is held by the examination for the position of clerk in Customs and Immigration for which 27,000 people competed on the same day.

The exams were the old-fashioned written kind and they had the symbolic significance of those high school matriculation exams. Naturally enough, cheating took place; the most obvious dodge was to have a more qualified friend take one's place. Others tried for some form of recommendation. According to a departmental financial officer: "Whole clans seemed to have been hired this way: the Toronto clan, the Alberta clan, and the British clan which swamped the technical and scientific ranks at some point." But generally, the principle of a universal examination was adhered to, and the general feeling was that the process was a fair one.

Political support for individual candidates seems to have been rare and not particularly desirable. "The Commission was so obsessed with political patronage that it had become taboo. There was patronage in the regions for unskilled seasonal jobs, but for the permanent staff of the public service, it was difficult," said a former employee.

"If by chance some poor fellow had been recommended by a member of Parliament, the Commission did its best to have that fact become known and to make the candidate pay later for his impertinence." However, the political personnel surrounding ministers was not very numerous, and at that time there was not the kind of back-and-forth movement between the political and bureaucratic orders, that exists nowadays.

However, this description may be unduly idealistic, according to some observers who say that human nature still prevailed in the bureaucracy and that exceptions to the rule were by no means rare. Their perceptions were confirmed, in 1958, with the publication of the Heeney Report which acknowledged the reality of political and bureaucratic favouritism.

They also point out that bureaucratic tasks were repetitive and made few demands on personal initiative. "The norm was for a letter to be done over six times, and it was much later that I finally grasped the reason for it. My superior insisted that each letter conform to the law without any ambiguity. The idea was not to interpret but to obey," confessed a former departmental head.

On the financial side, rigidity was law: no discretion was allowed. Any extra expenditures and any request which was not part of existing regulations had to go through the all-powerful Comptroller General of the Treasury. "No spending commitment could be entered into by a department unless the Comptroller's staff was satisfied that it was for the purpose intended by Parliament, when the funds were voted, that funds were in fact available during the fiscal year, and that the commitment was entered into by an authorized official."[39]

These ideas were implemented in the most minuscule details. Letterhead, onionskin and carbon paper were handed out to secretaries almost a sheet at a time. A pencil had to be worn down to the eraser before another one was issued. Taxis were out of the question, and only trains were used for business trips. Out of town business was usually organized in such a way that employees would be traveling on weekends and preparing their reports on the way home. To those who feel that the public service has deteriorated since then, it should be pointed out that these standards also applied to private enterprise. If a director in government service did not attend international conferences, travel first class and eat in the best restaurants, these amenities were also denied to the vice-president of a Toronto oil company who never had as much as a cup of coffee on his expense account.

The Other Side of the Coin

The penny-pinching of the postwar period would certainly please today's taxpayers who might wonder why the public service did not remain the way it was. . . which is the same as asking why Canada did not remain a country of small towns. It would be stating the obvious to say that the public service was no longer the same because Canada itself had changed. In fact, it changed so much that it could no longer stand these seemingly old, mean and stingy bureaucrats.

While it is true that many people remembering the 1950s say the public was awed and respectful of the mandarins, this seems to be an embellishment and a trick of memory rather than a reality, since archival research does not confirm this impression. The only exception to the general rule seems to be the Ottawa Journal which sang the praises of local heroes from time to time, and for this very reason deserves to be quoted. "The old ministers would go, the familiar names and voices; on hand to shepherd their successors, to show them what makes government tick, would be the civil service, those top-flight permanent officials of whom Canada, apart from an occasional and healthy thought about bureaucracy, has every reason to be proud."[40]

But this was an exception. As early as the mid fifties, the old structure started to groan and crack under the strain of a triple crisis of growth, authority and management.

Growth Crisis

The 1950s were not the years of timid conservatism, rooted in the social and economic status quo, that a great many people imagine. On the contrary, the social benefits which Canadians hold most dearly were either planned or implemented during this decade.

The political leaders of that period were more profoundly moved by the depression they had known than by the war in which few of them had actually served. They were determined to build a new Canada on the solid foundations described by economist John Meynard Keynes who at this point was more influential than all the mandarins put together.

35

"The period was one of affluence and optimism. It was believed that governments could, with the appropriate application of technology and deployment of resources, overcome economic and social maladies."[41] It is in this light that one must interpret the policy papers of 1946 urging the Canadian government to intervene aggressively in economic and technical domains.

In this same spirit the government launched a whole series of wide-ranging socio-economic programs: family allowances in 1945 and hospital insurance (in co-operation with the provinces) in 1948, which are now part of a complex social security system.

Finally, under the impetus of External Affairs Minister Lester B. Pearson, Canada was determined, partly because of economic interests and partly due to a desire for independence, to carve out a larger role for itself in international affairs. Accordingly, diplomatic representation abroad increased rapidly.

Everything had to be conceptualized, negotiated, planned and executed. Between 1950 and 1960 the public service grew from 127,196 to 157,013. It was a relatively modest increase compared to the enormous expansion of the immediate postwar period, but, it was selective and had a fundamental influence on later developments.

This growth was largely a professional one. It called on a great variety of specialists: engineers, agronomists, physicists, meteorologists, technicians, arts graduates for External Affairs, specialists in finance and administration, to the point that the Commission had to launch a recruiting program and scout university campuses. The supply of university graduates in the 1950s could hardly meet the demands of a country whose economy was undergoing rapid transformation. The Public Service Commission acknowledged the seriousness of the situation. "The past five years average demand of about 460 graduates and 900 undergraduates (for summer employment) was not met. Assignment averaged about 415 graduates over the same period. Thus the backlog of continuing positions for recent university graduates had grown to nearly 800 at the end of 1955. At the same time the estimated demand for undergraduates is up to 1,400."[42]

This means that between 1950 and 1955, the public service

absorbed 2,000 university graduates and needed another thousand. It was leaving behind the idea of service along quasi-military lines and moving towards a more professionally inspired type of organization. It thus became the largest employer of university graduates in the country, after the schools and the universities.

In the mid 1950s the atmosphere in the national capital began to change dramatically. It wasn't the heady sixties yet, because mentalities were still very much anchored in the past. But it appeared that the inherited bureaucratic structure could not adapt smoothly to the changes which the government was eager to bring about. The unthinkable happened: doubts arose concerning the mandarins.

Authority Crisis

For some of the newcomers to the public service, the very things that had been so commendable about the mandarins now became blameworthy. Everthing about them was critized.

o   Their age: senior bureaucrats were aging in the public as well as in the private sector. As early as 1956, the annual report of the Public Service Commission drew attention to the problem by referring to events south of the border: "A survey of business and government in the United States and Canada revealed that two in five of those holding executive posts are between 56 and 65 years of age and that fewer than one in ten are under 45."[43]

o   Their education: According to young public servants, they were "old-fashioned, inefficient, and in-bred. . . the generalist educations which had served them so well in forming an "overview" of the dramatic problems of the Depression and the war were inadequate, according to them, to deal with the intricacies of an expanding government in a technological age."[44]

o   Their esprit de corps was increasingly interpreted as the mark of an elitist and privileged caste.

o   Their prudence was seen as coldness towards Canadians who happened to be underprivileged. According to Christina Newman, "Ideologically, the mandarin is a drawing room liberal who expresses considerable concern for the underprivileged over

37

drinks. . . and fails to see the difference between good manners and compassion."[45]

o   Their self-effacing manners were interpreted as the supreme hypocrisy of a group of plotters who had once been characterized as "the gang of eight."[46]

The mandarins were condemned for their dress (so old-fashioned), for living in Rockcliffe (so dull), their restaurants (so Canadian), and their habit of serving meatloaf for dinner (so provincial!).

Finally, they were accused of remaining passive towards the administration of the public service which, at the end of the 1950s was literally choking on its own procedures and regulations and grinding to a crippling halt.

Management Crisis

Hubert Laframboise acknowledged the growing management crisis: "The years 1945-60 were not a golden age of administrative reform. In retrospect, it is plain that we neglected to move quickly, if at all, in such matters as employee relations, bilingualism, program budgeting and large-scale systems analysis. In particular, management consultants in government, as a rule, failed to raise their sights to major problems requiring solution. Attached to, and ensnared by, the concept that their duty lay in responding to requests and not initiating reform, they spent much of their time helping managers to swat flies while failing to communicate to them that the foundations of their over-all administrative systems were being eaten by termites."[47]

There were two bottlenecks threatening the complete paralysis of government machinery: finance and personnel.

The budget prepared for each fiscal year left no room at all for any kind of initiative, so that the expansion of certain areas of government was painful, if not actually impossible. Any expenditure had to go through accounting procedures taking up weeks, if not months, eventually overcoming the best intentions in the world. When Grant Glassco was asked to head a royal commission on these matters, he found "within each department. . . universal frustration with the irksome system of control that stultified the initiative of departmental managers. Similarly, (he) found most departments had in recent years been strengthening their internal machinery for attending to their own domestic requirements. . . by and large, the control orientation rather than the servicing motive of the central agencies brought them into constant conflict with the department's own housekeeping units."[48]

One couldn't help making the comparison with the private sector where budgeting in the early sixties was geared to credit and initiative. According to a former member of the public service, never did this organization seem more reactionary, behind the times, out of touch with reality, than at this time. "The traditional annual cash budgets were condemned as. . . irrational, because they dealt with inputs instead of outputs; short-sighted because they cover only one year. . . fragmented, because as a rule only changes are reviewed. . ."[49]

As for personnel management, it just went from bad to worse. In 1946 the Gordon Commission had complained of the "considerable delays in making appointments and promotions at all levels of the service." It often took a year, and sometimes more, before a position could be offered to a candidate. The everpresent fear of political patronage, the centralization of staffing, the meagre resources of the Commission, the overwork resulting from the return of the war veterans, all these things contributed to making the system inordinately slow.

"By the mid 1950s, centralized personnel administration began to break down under its own weight. Cumbersome staffing procedures could not respond quickly enough to secure talent in a continually tight employment market. The system of across-the-board salary increases was a sluggish, undifferentiated, and often inaccurate attempt to maintain a competitive position in the labour market, and to retain staff in the face of attractive opportunities in the prosperous private sector. An increasingly professionalized management cadre in departments fretted under the restrictions imposed on them."[50] It was impossible to avoid the comparison with private enterprise which was engaged in the competitive recruitment of the cream of the nation's young university graduates. The general impression was that the public service could not keep the talented specialists it needed longer than six months. It should be added that demand in the private sector was so strong at the time that the government seemed to attract only the discards from business.

The Troops Lag Behind

In addition to these administrative difficulties and to changing mentalities, the public service faced another serious problem: while the government had always thought of itself as being in the forefront of progress regarding employee remuneration, it was now falling behind the private sector to such an extent that even the ultra-conservative Civil Service Commission had to broach the subject in its Annual Report for 1955. "It will be necessary to keep comparing the benefits of the Civil Service and outside employment. In the years since the war industrial employers have continually been raising the 'ante' in the form of fringe benefits, partly to entice scarce manpower and partly by way of concessions to the unions. No longer are Civil Service benefits clearly more liberal. Profit sharing, or incentive bonus plans, low-cost lunches, employer-contributory insurance plans, and car allowances are some of the benefits available with the industrial employers, but not in the service."[51]

Above all, the ponderous remuneration system, which rested on outdated conceptions and which was stratified into more than 2,000 categories, was no longer able to keep up with an economy which had already become inflationary at the end of the war. Between 1947 and 1948, the cost-of-living index jumped by 19.5 per cent. Employee associations, which had always tried to maintain their distance from the union movement, could no longer accept low pay for the honour of serving their country. The average salary in 1955 was $3,108, up from $1,873 in 1946 and this was not quite equal to the average wage in some parts of the country. For many subordinate employees, and particularly for temporary ones, monthly wages barely covered the rent, so that moonlighting was widespread.

The possibility of reform was brought up, but discussions were extremely slow and dragged on throughout the 1950s. They led to the establishment of the Pay Research Bureau whose mandate was to provide effective terms of comparison between public and private sector remuneration. In a sense, the government was giving symbolic recognition to the professionalism of its own employees: the civil service was in its death throes and the public service was ready to be born.

Nevertheless, the fifties ended without too much of a stir. The difficult transition from a wartime to a peacetime economy had been successfully managed by the Canadian government. The war veterans had come home, and ten per cent of them had been integrated into the public service where they could age quietly without any worries. As a result, in 1961 almost 60 per cent of the personnel in government was over forty years old.

Nobody has ever bothered to ask what would have happened had the government not opened the doors of the public service to a large contingent of war veterans, and the question does not interest anyone today. In any case, after it was over, the times were not ripe for intellectual dissertations on history. The sixties had arrived. Let's have a party!

2: TAKE-OFF

Ottawa-Hull 1960

The sixties began without fanfare: in January of that year the national capital, now numbering 420,000 inhabitants, seemed calmer than ever, except perhaps on Parliament Hill, where John Diefenbaker, who had been in power for three years, was keeping everyone on edge.

Not that the country was doing all that well: twelve per cent inflation, seven per cent unemployment, the obsolescence of the public service, and the wartime public debt were sources of concern for everyone.

Yet Canadians were better off than ever before: the average weekly wage had risen from $45 in 1950 to $76 in 1960. The improvement was all the more appreciated since the memory of the war and of the depression lingered on. The majority of Canadians could now afford to give their children what they themselves had not necessarily enjoyed: proper shelter, food and education. They did not hesitate to make the most of it: according to the 1961 census, 7.5 million people in Canada were below the age of twenty, and 5 million under ten years old. The baby boom was under way.

Still this aging public service remained clogged by the recruitment of veterans who no longer had any raison d'être. The government no longer had to prepare for war and had no intention of using the 30,000 employees of the Department of Defence (a quarter of the public service) for anything other than a paper war. The best it could do was to wait patiently for the inevitable attrition through retirement which was imminent for twenty per cent of the personnel in the ranks of the public service. Logically speaking, the situation could be expected to improve: the public service, which people said was grossly overweight, would soon begin to slim down, take on some bright young specialists, and modernize its operations.

But these expectations overlooked the three main elements which shattered the backward-looking dreams of a handful of managers.

The first element, a relatively harmless one, is the propensity of any large organization to automatically fill any void unless cutbacks are specifically and peremptorily ordered by the executive. Directors and bosses are never eager to trim their empires, habit having acquired force of law and rendering every position necessary and justifiable. Furthermore, even when growth has been artificial, the entire organization will transform itself in such a way as to accommodate this growth and administer it, creating a new structure which makes everything seem necessary. This proposition was brilliantly demonstrated by Parkinson as well as by the British television series "Yes Minister" in which a hospital without any patients or doctors (there were no funds available to welcome the first) is a hive of administrative activity keeping everything in tip-top shape: "the best in the service," according to the inimitable Sir Humphrey.

The second element, a much more weighty one, is the propensity of modern government to transform itself into a social and economic leviathan generating massive employment opportunities for the conceptualization and administration of its new ventures. In Canada, Keynes' influence, "woven into the policy fabric of senior economic departments such as Finance, provided the basis for active state intervention."[1] Towards the end of the 1950s, Canadians asked the state to provide exactly what the latter was eager to propose in the elections of 1957: countless initiatives which heretofore had been the handiwork of Adam Smith's invisible hand and of equally ethereal divine providence.

The third somewhat more hypothetical element, was the necessity for the Canadian government to act as a social safety valve for the second time, and open the doors of the public service to a part of the seven and a half million young Canadians of the baby boom generation. After 1960, they were hitting the labour market in wave after wave, and certainly could never have all been absorbed by the private sector. But unlike the wartime decision, which was entirely clear, this one was taken less consciously with a view to expanding the field of government intervention even further. As we shall see, the new wave was not composed of disciplined and conservative veterans. The new wave was boiling over with energy and ideas. It was ready to transform what had been a bureaucratic organization into an active government.

The Young Warriors: Who Were They?

A British historian has compared them to the barbarians who precipitated the fall of the Roman Empire. One should read in this comparison more than a sarcastic reference to the fact that the first wave of the baby boom, the hippies, looked very much like the hordes surrounding Attila the Hun. History teaches us that each generation has its wild youth: the Italian duellists of the Renaissance who wore more pearls than any single oyster bed could ever produce, the Incroyables and the Merveilleuses under the French Directory, the British Dandies of the 19th century. But these episodes were ephemeral and localized; they had no other social consequence than providing subject matter for the literary chroniclers of their time. Past societies had two formidable ways of dealing with young people who failed to toe the proper social line: religious orders or the army.

In the case of the baby boom, and considering only its impact on the labour market, it was clear for any demographer, even an amateur one, that Canada was headed for some turbulent years. The wave of young people that was about to overrun the country was totally unlike anything that had been experienced in the past.

First of all it was not an ordinary wave but a tidal wave which was without historical precedent, or, if there had been any, one can suppose that it had been decimated through infant mortality. We tend to forget that as late as the 19th century a newborn child in Canada had only one chance in two of ever reaching its fifth birthday. This was certainly not the case with the baby boom generation. For the first time a large mass of children would become a large mass of adults as a result of the progress achieved in hygiene and nutrition. Canada beat all the demographic records of modern countries: the baby boom here was the biggest and the longest. In 1961, 42 per cent of all Canadians were younger than twenty, and 34 per cent were younger than fifteen. Canada was the youngest country in the Organization for Economic Co-operation and Development.

For the first time there was no question of sending the surplus of young people into the army or into the religious orders which were still thriving in Quebec. This generation, brought up in a climate of affluence, inclined towards hedonism, and an ideological viewpoint which certainly did not include war. It also leaned towards agnosticism and towards the rejection of traditional religious values.

Strangely enough, some of those orders that had survived many vicissitudes over the centuries were helpless before this new postwar generation, which had received an education different from that of its predessors, one that was based on faith in science and social progress.

This was the first generation to receive, as a group, the kind of education that had once been reserved for a social minority and for one sex alone. In 1956, there were barely 16,600 university degrees awarded; that number reached 49,300 in 1966, and more than 96,500 in 1976.[2]

The majority of these degree were in the arts, social sciences, economics, political science and education. 40 per cent of the degrees awarded between 1961 and 1971 were in the arts, and 20 per cent in education. At the MA level, the trend was even more pronounced: 70 per cent of the student population were specializing in fields of studies where existing professional outlets were limited to two broad categories:

o   education where needs were particularly acute because of the unusually large number of children in the second and third waves of the baby boom;

o   political, social and economic analysis, where the need was great
     because governments in the early sixties were stepping up their
     activities in this direction.

The baby boomers, however, did not wait to be invited into these
new jobs. They aggressively forced the issue. Their education, the
general economic well-being of the country, the absence of material
concerns, and the enthusiasm characteristic of young people, all
contributed to an ideology of government which was based on five broad
principles:[3]

1 -   A just society is an egalitarian one.
2 -   Tradition is bad because it often goes against equality.
3 -   Economics and the social sciences are the instruments of social
       change.
4 -   Government is the ideal instrument to bring about the social and
       economic reforms necessary for a just society.
5 -   Civil servants have a social and economic mission.

"Thus the altruistic technocrat was born."[4]

The Capture of Ottawa

Any analysis of the impact of the baby boomers on the bureaucratic
labour market between 1965 and 1975 is speculation for the most part.
There is some sketchy information on this topic, but not enough to
permit a systematic study of the demographic revolution which
transformed the country's social and economic structures. The irony of
the situation is that this highly educated generation simply neglected to
observe itself. According to a contemporary demographer, political and
bureaucratic decision-makers were guilty of the same oversight: "Most
of them did not know that there had been a baby boom, or if they did,
they did not give it the importance it deserved."

During the 1960s, the public service was not fully computerized,
so that data on this question are either non-existent, incompatible,
incomplete or unreliable. It is impossible to know precisely how the
baby boomers or university graduates invaded sectors of the public
service, at what levels they entered, or in what academic disciplines
they worked. At best, we have some indications which can be provided

by the university recruitment program and by MRIS (Mangement Resources Integrated System).

In spite of these statistical limitations, it is still possible to advance some general comments.

First, as Table 2 indicates, the public service hired more than its share of baby boomers, just as it had hired more than its share of war veterans. In 1961, by the time the veterans had been fully absorbed, the average age in the public service was higher than that of the labour force as a whole. By 1981, when "Operation Baby Boom" was over, the average age in the public service was lower than that in the labour force. With its quarter million employees and its great occupational diversity, the public service can be considered to be representative of the labour force.

The infusion of young blood was particularly strong in the national capital. As Table 3 indicates in 1984, the 25-44 age group constituted, almost 64 per cent of all permanent government employees.

Secondly members of the baby boom generation with university degrees beat a well-worn path to the door of the Public Service Commission, as Table 4 indicates. In 1977, a record year, almost a

Table 2: Labour Force and Public Service by age groups, in percentages, 1961 and 1981

	1961		1981	
Age	Labour Force %	Public Service %	Labour Force %	Public Service %
15-24	21.7	11.3	23.6	9.8
25-44	45.8	50.2	48.4	56.1
45-64	32.5	38.5	28.0	34.1

Sources: Statistics Canada, Annual Reports of the Civil Service Commission and of the Public Service Commission.

Table 3: Permanent Employment, National Capital Region, Public Service, by age groups, 1984

Age	Numbers
15-19	54
20-24	3,234
25-29	9,228
30-34	12,325
35-39	12,054
40-44	8,343
45-49	6,583
50-54	6,188
55-59	4,869
60-64	3,096
65 and over	111
Total	66,085

Source: Public Service Commission, unpublished data.

quarter of the university graduates in Canada filed job applications with the federal government.

Obviously these figures are significant inasmuch as one can weed out all frivolous and routine applications. Students are prone to send out their curriculum vitae to as many places as possible, and the federal government happened to be the best known employer. Nevertheless, these figures are remarkable in light of the fact that the federal public service accounts for only three per cent of the Canadian labour force. According to a recruiting agent of the day, the prevailing feeling was that the public service had a moral duty to offer professional outlets to young people, just as it had seemed fitting earlier that veterans should be hired as a matter of policy.

But most of all, the federal public service had become the largest employer of university graduates after the educational system itself. The first reliable data in this respect are found in the Annual Reports of the Civil Service Commission. In 1961, 9,500 university graduates, B.A. and higher, were working in the federal service, which is one employee out of fourteen. A study by the Pay Research Bureau says nothing about the graduates' fields of studies but it does indicate to what departments they were assigned. It is possible to conclude that

Table 4: Applications under the Post-secondary Recruitment Program,
         1967 to 1977

	All programs		
			Rate of
	Student	Number of	Penetration
Year	Population	Applications	(in percentages)
1967	49,271	5,926	12.0
1968	55,535	8,738	15.7
1969	62,838	8,719	13.9
1970	70,289	5,172	7.4
1971	78,363	6,431	8.2
1972	84,546	12,367	14.6
1973	83,255	18,993	22.8
1974	86,943	18,362	21.1
1975	93,645	19,230	20.5
1976	96,524	21,124	21.9
1977	102,575	25,027	24.4

Source: An Examination of the Administrative Trainee Program,
         Working Paper, Public Service Commission, November 1978.

the majority were medical and scientific personnel. "As an example, the Department of Agriculture has 2,187 university graduates and the Department of Mines and Technical Surveys, 688. Of those with professional accounting certificates, 1,050 in all, 866 were in the Department of National Revenue and all but 18 of the 1,733 nurses were employed in the Departments of Veterans Affairs and National Health and Welfare."[5]

The trend was even more pronounced in the national capital for which the incomplete MRIS data indicate that among employees born between 1930 and 1940, there were at least 400 Ph. D.s and 560 M.A.s. And the trend was sustained as long as the government broadened its socio-economic activities.

Thirdly, did the public service absorb more than its share of Canadian university graduates? This is very likely, although the claim is based mainly on the perceptions of people who were active in Ottawa during that period. They claim there was an "invasion" of university graduates.

According to official figures the federal government hired less than its share: one per cent of all university graduates, whereas it accounts for three per cent of the labour force. However, these figures are incomplete since they apply only to students who were hired under the university recruitment program. They do not account for those who were hired directly by a department, either on a temporary basis which later became permanent or immediately on a permanent basis. Later, the Clark-Zsigmond study provided more precise information. It came to the conclusion that the public service (as defined by Statistics Canada and including the armed forces and Crown corporations) had absorbed a substantial proportion of university graduates in 1976: especially in political science (15 per cent), psychology (8.2 per cent), sociology (8.4 per cent), humanities (6.3 per cent), French literature (6.3 per cent), and history (7.6 per cent).

Again later, the official yet incomplete MRIS data show how extensive recruitment was in the social and related sciences in the national capital. There were 473 economists, 230 political scientists, 555 commerce and business graduates, 307 arts graduates, 211 historians, 128 psychologists and 112 sociologists, all born between 1940 and 1950, working for the public service in Ottawa-Hull in 1984, and most likely hired during the 1960s.

The total for these academic disciplines alone is 2,000 graduates, but given the considerable number of unknown factors in the study they may well have been twice that number. Furthermore, 82 per cent of these graduates were male and they represented 17 per cent of all male federal employees born between 1940 and 1950.

Last of all, these young graduates had a career very different from that of their elders. Those who took part in administrative training programs enjoyed, for the most part, a dazzling rise to the top. In 1977, while they were still under the age of 35 and had fewer than ten years of continuous service, one quarter on average had reached the top levels in their group, as Table 5 shows.

More general examples are possible beyond 1976 and 1977, when the first reliable computerized data become available. There is a large proportion of people between 35 and 39 years old at the top of

Table 5:   Recruitment of Trainees in Administration, Public Service

| | Year of Recruitment | | | | | |
| | 1967-1977 | | 1967-1972 | | 1973-1977 | |
	No.	%	No.	%	No.	%
Senior Executive	7	0.5	7	1.1	–	–
Senior Management (excl. SX)	303	20.2	297	46.4	6	0.7
Feeders to Senior Management	170	11.3	103	16.1	67	7.8
Others	849	56.6	233	36.4	616	71.6
AT	171	11.4	–	–	171	19.9
Total	1500	100.0	640	100.0	860	100.0

Source: An Examination of the Administrative Trainee Program, Public Service Commission, November 1978.

each group. Although statistical evidence is lacking, it is more than likely that these people were hired during the second half of the 1960s when they were between 25 and 30 years old. It is more than likely, as well, that a large number were university graduates and employed in the national capital region.

And a Wind of Reform Arose
It is self-evident that the mentality of these newcomers completely altered even the physical aspect of the bureaucracy which evolved in complete harmony with the mood of the country. These were years of enthusiasm which passed like a charm. The high point was the celebrated Expo 67 in Montreal, visited by 50,000,000 people during a period of six months, which Peter Newman has described as "one of those rare moments that change the direction of a nation's history."[6]

The rising stars of that day, who have now reached the top of the bureaucracy and are aging more or less gracefully, remember those years as a golden age during which everything was possible. Those were the years one could be happy in the public service, not only because of the material advantages, but also because of an open-mindedness, a dynamism and the feeling of being useful and of helping to build a just society. This was a Canada that was in better health, better housed and better educated: a Canada that had self-confidence.

It is easy to be cynical in the light of 1985, but it would be unjust to cast doubts on the sincerity of those who wanted things to be better for all, who wanted to share. One has to wait for the 1970s to see the idea of "always better" being transformed into a harsher "always more."

The 1960s were generous and euphoric years, all too trusting and without fear. They were years during which the public service:

o grew rapidly as new social and economic programs were being implemented;

o was reorganized to foster the initiative and consultation necessary for expanded services;

o management was rejuvenated;

o gave human nature a blank cheque, neglecting to build in safety precautions, alarm systems and mechanisms for the correction of errors.

Expansion of New Sectors

Between 1960 and 1968, the public service grew by 54 per cent, from 130,000 to almost 200,000 employees. Once again, growth was not uniform: it mirrored the new directions in government policy.

The manifesto for government action for the decade ahead was proclaimed in 1960. It had been drafted not by the government, but by the Liberal Party which was still in the Opposition at that time. It proclaimed three basic priorities: "Regional disparities, manpower policies and social services."[7] When Lester B. Pearson came to power in April 1963, the manifesto "provided him with a sizeable portion of his government's program during the rest of the decade."[8]

Following this manifesto, there appeared a whole series of programs geared to social and economic issues which are among the most important in modern Canadian history: medicare in 1966, collective bargaining for federal employees in 1967, and the manpower allowances program in 1968. On the political side, the federal government was committed to a larger degree of centralization and determined to use its fiscal powers to correct regional disparities.

53

New departments were created: Forests in 1960, Industry in 1963, and Consumer Affairs in 1966. The powers of other departments were considerably expanded: the Solicitor General ceased to be an appendage of Justice, and Manpower and Immigration were merged. Others ballooned under new responsibilities. For example, between 1962 and 1969, Agriculture went from 6,125 to 10,091 employees, National Health and Welfare from 3,053 to 6,114, External Affairs from 1,574 to 2,178, and Mines from 2,514 to 4,628.

It was inevitable. The new sectors of activity could hardly be mapped out and expected to prosper within the old administrative structures whose philosophy—in financial matters, particularly—was based on the preservation of the status quo. Administrative reforms were needed as much as a new type of manager, not only to oversee the new programs, but to participate in their conception, articulation, integration and co-ordination. The time had come for initiative.

Making Room for Initiative

In spite of the suspicions he harboured towards bureaucrats, John Diefenbaker was well aware of how badly government machinery needed modernization. The Comptroller of the Treasury, although a "big-time spender" compared to W.C. Ronson, continued to tighten the purse strings just as everyone else wanted to loosen them. Ministers and managers were worn out by the administrative wrangling necessary to replace a pencil, organize a conference, or create a new post.

In 1960, the "Chief" asked Grant Glassco to head a Royal Commission with a mandate "to promote greater efficiency" in public affairs. 160 researchers were hired, half of whom were associated with management consulting firms while the other half were from the top levels of private enterprise. The old mandarins had been completely shut out, word had it that they could not have anything worthwhile to contribute to a new administrative philosophy oriented towards the future. Glassco wanted to demonstrate "how professionally—competent, independent reviewers can find innovative, imaginative, and common-sense improvements and solutions—probably of an order that could not reasonably be expected to be generated internally."[9]

Given the composition of the Commission and its staff, no one was surprised at the nature of the recommendations it published two years later in five heavy tomes. The report was the bible of those who put in motion the great administrative reforms of that decade. According to one observer, they were "probably responsible for more significant changes in the personnel function of the service than any other event since Confederation, with the possible exception of the modern Civil Service Commission in 1918."[10]

"Management to the Managers" was the Commission's byword. This apparent tautology hit Ottawa like a shower in the desert. What it proposed was simply to lighten staffing and financial controls in order to provide managers with greater decision-making latitude.

Indeed, the report "slashed"[11] the centralized staffing and hiring procedures of the Civil Service Commission and proposed an almost total delegation of staffing authority to the departments. The idea was accepted. The Civil Service Commission tried to resist. It lost the battle as well as its name: it was henceforth known as the Public Service Commission.

But the reform with the most far-reaching consequences was undoubtedly the one affecting finances. "Traditionally, departments requested and received funds on the basis of standard objects of expenditure. The budgeting system was control oriented, in that the main purpose of the exercise was to contain the increases from year to year in these objects of expenditure on a department-to-department basis. No consideration was given and little information generated on the objectives and rationale of the programs for which the money was spent. In 1962, the Glassco Commission recommended that departmental estimates be prepared on the basis of programs of activity and that long-term plans of expenditure requirements also be submitted by departments."[12] Once again the proposal was well received, and the public service adopted a so-called positive management approach to public finances. The Treasury Board's responsibility became co-ordination rather than control, advising rather than ordering. Thus perished the watchdog of the public purse. What happened then was that departments were given free rein; their spending could increase year by year inasmuch as they could justify future programs.

This kind of justification is no problem for any manager worth his salt. Without giving away the story's ending, the reader can easily guess the conclusions reached in the 1977 interim report by the Federal-Provincial Relations Office. "On the basis of the costs and financial resource operation information provided by departments for the present study it appears that most programs grew very quickly without assessment of the impact of these programs." [13]

It explains in bureaucratic terminology that certain programs were useless and costly, and that there had been a large number of them. As one observer said, "The whole period was given to improvisation. Everybody wanted to create new things. People competed as to who would come out with the most innovative and brilliant idea. When I look back on it now, it was utter madness."

The frenzy also affected organizational expenses in ministers' offices and in government services. Extravagance was written into the bills that came in for conferences, travelling, office redecoration and outside consultants. National Health and Welfare, for instance, hired a team of "creative writers."

W.C. Ronson would have turned over in his grave at the thought of these follies. Today, they would trigger a wave of hostility towards the public service which would be perfectly justified were it not for the fact that public extravagance was rather small potatoes compared to what might have been found in the highly prosperous private sector if the auditor general had had access to their accounts. These were the days of the national potlatch, days when it would have been unacceptable for the public sector to lag behind. But the excuse is still a flimsy one.

Some people were already beginning to feel that public servants had obviously lost their heads. They had committed themselves to an irresponsible course, one that did not take into account the specific character of the public service, a course without the final bottom line found in private enterprise profit or bankruptcy. It would be unjust to put the blame for this thoughtlessness on Glassco himself, since he had the good sense to propose a review committee independent of the public service to provide an outside assessment of spending programs. However, this was one of the few recommendations to be ignored. The desire to be free of administrative shackles was so strong that no one was prepared to trade old regulations for new ones, particularly if wielded by people outside the bureaucratic structure. Consequently, there was no check on public spending, and no appraisal. There was little fear of bankruptcy, everyone acted on the assumption that public funds were inexhaustible.

Making Room for Consultation

Meanwhile, in 1962 the government came to the conclusion that its 137,000 employees could no longer be treated as a group apart from the labour force, as people whose status was somewhere between that of domestic servants and army personnel. There were growing pressures to allow public servants the same rights as those enjoyed in the private sector. Similarly, it was thought that public servants should become more representative of the country as a whole, beginning with French Canada.

Francophones had without any doubt been treated as second class citizens in the public service. They had been almost completely rejected during the period of the great mandarins. According to J.L. Granatstein: "Not only were Québécois not represented at the very top, but they were also denied a share of power at lower levels. For example a report on employees in Finance noted on January 8, 1940 that there were no French Canadians in the Deputy Minister's Office, only 17 (out of 145) in the Administration Branch and 6 (out of 65) in the Accounts Branch. More than a dozen years later, in 1953, John Porter's study of the bureaucratic élite noted that French Canadians held only 13.4 per cent of the top posts in the public service."[14] In 1960, as the Quiet Revolution was getting underway in Quebec, very little had changed. However, demands for improvements were mounting, and in 1963 Lester B. Pearson set up the Royal Commission on Bilingualism and Biculturalism. Its conclusions were the basis for all future policies on these matters.

The Public Service Commission stepped up its language training programs and established a complex job classification system so that bilingualism would become a reality. Between 1964 and 1973, there were 42,190 enrolments in the Commission's French language courses. The Secretary of State translation services employed a thousand people. The total cost between 1970 and 1977 came to about two billion dollars for results that were more symbolic than real in terms of anglophones using French.[15]

But here again, any negative judgment on the effectiveness of the whole operation must be tempered by its socio-political character, another indication that the objectives of the public service cannot be modelled on those of private enterprise. The creation of a bilingual public service was a political decision whose effectiveness can only be assessed in terms of the country's political future.

Collective bargaining for the public service was another political decision, but electorally inspired. The 1963 elections promised to be very close, giving additional weight to the several hundred thousand votes cast by government employees. John Diefenbaker and Lester Pearson both saw the situation in the same light. In 1961 a new Civil Service Act had given employee associations and unions the legal right to consult central control agencies on a wide range of topics. This had taken several years to achieve, not because the government was dragging its feet but because the classification system was inextricable.[16]

The whole issue was quickly resolved without arousing the protests associated with earlier attempts. The reason was a simple one: the government had granted such large salary increases that those who had been downgraded were fully compensated. The public service was divided into six socio-professional categories, subdivided into groups, which were then subdivided, on an average, into three hierarchical levels.

The only contentious issue was the right to strike, but with elections fast approaching this was readily granted.

On February 23, 1967, Royal assent was given to an Act on Labour Relations in the Public Service establishing the collective bargaining process. The old-fashioned servants—soldiers without uniforms disappeared. They became full-fledged Canadian workers. They were well paid, all the more so since, while sharing the same advantages with other workers, they didn't face the same risks.

The Great Euphoria

But who was talking about risks in 1968? The decade flowed by like a charm, and so rapidly that at the time no one anticipated the repercussions of the changes that had taken place. The times were geared to action, so much so that any questioning or hesitation was deemed to be reactionary. The mandarins of the old school kept their peace and retired discreetly, sometimes hurt, sometimes exasperated, often worried at the turn of events.

They hardly recognized the city which had provided a backdrop for their talents. The bureaucratic explosion had changed the physical aspect of Ottawa forever. Between 1965 and 1969, the number of civil servants rose from 38,094 to 48,754, figures which do not include the large number of people on contract (the new temporary employees), those working for temporary agencies, seasonal workers, or the whole range of government consultants with newly opened offices.

The old downtown buildings could no longer house all the troops. External Affairs left the old Langevin Block in 1973 for the Pearson Building on Sussex Drive. National Health and Welfare and Statistics Canada moved to Tunney's Pasture, the windiest strip in Ottawa. The staff of the Communications Department had better luck: they were relocated downtown. Everywhere offices were new, with open spaces, and—how symbolic!—sealed from any contact with the outside world. Too hot in winter, too cold in summer, they were forever recycling the same stale air. Restaurants and real estate thrived.

It wasn't opulence yet, and for many people Ottawa remained "too dowdy to be true." But slowly the city grew and prospered. The salary increases awarded in 1967 helped a great deal, but there was more to it than that. Promotions, an indirect form of salary increase, had been very rare in the past but had now become the norm, as shown in Table 6. They went from 14 per cent of all appointments in 1952 to a staggering 34 per cent in 1970.

Table 6:   Appointments, Departures and Promotions in the Public
Service of Canada 1964, 1965, 1966, 1967

	1964	1965	1966	1967
Employees under the Employment in the Public Service Act	138,666	140,206	145,783	200,329*
New Appointments	19,199	21,700	21,979	31,293
Departures	13,162	14,546	14,343	16,830
Promotions	18,536	20,475	18,749	30,088

*   Includes employees at prevailing rates and ships' officers and crews
coming under the Employment in the Public Service Act, on March
13, 1967.

Source: Public Service Commission, Annual Report 1968.

The proportion of appointments, already extraordinarily high, was
probably still higher in the national capital where upper and middle
levels are over-represented. For example, at the highest level of the
hierarchy (SX), promotions represented almost 61 per cent of all
appointments in 1966, as shown in Table 7.

Table 7:   New Appointments at the Executive Level in the Public
Service of Canada, 1966

New Appointments	34
Between departments	23
Promotions within the public service	88
Total	145

Source: Public Service Commission, Annual Report 1970

But this group was not even the most upwardly mobile in Ottawa,
far from it. For example, young trainees in administration could expect
one promotion every two years, if not two or three promotions as in the
case of one candidate who joined the mandarin group at the tender age

of 23. A number of people younger than 30, and even 25, were traced to the SX levels of the bureaucracy.

The consequences of such a high rate of promotion among young people were numerous and irreversible. The first one is obvious. The decision-makers became younger, to a point where one may infer that the management of certain government programs was handed over to totally inexperienced people, whose mentality was likely to be spendthrift. The bureaucratic mentality during the 1960s (and this includes the majority in the hierarchy) saw promotions as a normal part of life in the public service and spared no effort to obtain them. Another important consequence was that a young, well-educated bureaucratic bourgeoisie was beginning to settle into the public service.

A Twitch of Nervousness

Yet there were a few clouds in the sky. The expansion of the federal public service was becoming too obvious not to be a source of concern. The Commission's report for 1967 announced that the number of government employees had passed the 200,000-mark. This round number was somehow frightening. On March 6, 1968 the government announced a freeze and even attempted a modest purge. It affected 888 employees, most of whom were transferred elsewhere. In 1970, however, the Commission's Annual Report proudly announced that the number of government employees had decreasd by 1,019.

But it was just a twitch, a trace of fear that quickly dissipated, a pause more than a stop. Indeed, the public service was on the point of getting its second wind, a second gust of delirium. . . all in the name of reason. Pierre Elliott Trudeau was coming to power.

3: FLYING HIGH

Folie à trois

History, according to a celebrated historian, is just the story of destiny. Events of the past, seen from the vantage point of the present, always seem necessary and always give the impression of complementing each other. The story of the Canadian government during the 1960s and the 1970s conforms to what might very well be an optical illusion: everything seemed to be in place to launch the country towards its difficult economic destiny.

On one hand, we have the federal public service which, as a result of the circumstantial growth of the postwar period, had to give up some of the central controls restricting staffing and spending and open its mind to the spirit of enterprise and innovation. But what is enterprise if not the ability to conquer a larger market, and what is a larger market for the public service but more services and spending programs?

On the other hand, by happy coincidence, we have the customers: the Canadian public, always eager for more services. There seemed to be plenty of money in the public kitty to pay for them. And the salesmen were there too: a whole generation of specialists with a great deal of imagination, a generation that had never known war and privation (the first one in the history of the industrialized countries to be so blessed), and for whom money was no object when it came to ideas.

The only element missing in all these coincidences was the catalyst who could represent and propel national aspirations. Indeed, at that very moment, there was in the cabinet of the aging Lester Pearson one of those men who are so perfectly in tune with their time that history assumes their dimensions. That man was the Minister of Justice, Pierre Elliott Trudeau.

He had everything to please the public in 1968, which happened to be a difficult year for wealthy industrialized countries: the "youth revolution" was on everyone's mind[1], whether quiet as in Quebec or violent as in Europe.

He was not that young himself, but he appeared to be so. He was francophone but seemed to be anglophone. He had had a traditional education in the humanities, but he believed in progress, in the social sciences and in cybernetics. He claimed to be a citizen of the world, but he was a nationalist. It was the perfect mixture for a generation steeped in the past and filled with dreams of the future. They made their sentiments known by bringing him to power in April 1968.

It was the crowning event of the tremendous growth of the Pearson years, duly sustained by three agents: the public, the political establishment and the bureaucracy, all three bound in an iron triangle. The first became more eager for new programs, the second was eager to promise even more than had been asked, and the third prospered and multiplied, adding its own requests to a list that was already quite long. To determine responsibility would be a lost cause, like trying to determine who is responsible for lung disease: smokers, tobacco manufacturers who incite them to smoke, or the government which imposes no discipline and which profits from taxes on tabacco.

Canadians may console themselves by saying the trend was common to all advanced industrial countries. "Government became a sort of unlimited liability insurance company, in the business of insuring all people at all times for every conceivable risk." The general view was that any problem could be solved "if only adequate structures and processes were put in place."[2] At the end of the 1960s, the citizens of all the wealthy countries of the world had managed to exchange authoritarian and demanding paternalism for an apparently

64

Table 8:   Total spending on public administration, as a percentage of the gross national product, in 1954 and 1973

	1954	1973
West Germany	31.9	40.5
Australia	--	27.0
Denmark	22.9	41.2
United States	26.9	31.1
France	34.9	43.4
Italy	28.5	37.7
Japan	23.2	22.1
Netherlands	31.4	49.0
United Kingdom	34.0	40.7

Source: Organization for Economic Co-operation and Development, National Accounts.

inexhaustible protective maternalism.   The public service everywhere grew accordingly, as Table 8 shows.

Of course, there were variations and exceptions from one country to another.   The traditions associated with the great schools of administration in Europe and the political traditions of the United States account for some of the differences.   But the main characteristics of the movement were shared by all. Canada, freer and younger, stood out by going to extremes, by being "distinctive in flavour."[3]   It became a much envied model for other countries at the beginning of the seventies.[4]

On taking power, Pierre Trudeau was determined to make the federal bureaucracy the spearhead of a modern Canada. In fact, for the first time in the history of the public service, the Prime Minister was interested in its internal operations. It is symptomatic that, in their respective memoirs, John Diefenbaker and Lester Pearson failed to devote even a single page to the hundreds of thousands of employees of whom they happened to be the executive heads. True, their successor had little interest in the individual clerk or in the application of the merit principle.   But he gave considerable thought to the question of process and to recruiting young new elites, more so than any of his predecessors or his opposite numbers in other industrialized countries. Canada had more (or worse, some would say) than mere bureaucrats: it had, in the words of Richard Gwyn, the Trudeaucrats.

Pas de deux

When Pierre Elliott Trudeau took over the Prime Minister's Office in the imposing Langevin Block on that April morning in 1968, he encountered what he hated most: a great administrative mess whose outward sign was an overflow of books and papers. It didn't mean that people worked badly or poorly, but on many occasions some brilliant improvisations were required. Yet this was a way of doing things which suited Lester B. Pearson who enjoyed putting his intellectual resources on the line and making use of his vast fund of bureaucratic knowledge. In the words of Marc Lalonde, he "was used to flying by the seat of his pants."[5]

According to some observers, the new Prime Minister was very much aware, more so than he showed, of the gaps in his knowledge of the system. Moreover, his education at the hands of the Jesuits at Brébeuf College had taught him to distrust the intuitive approach which was deemed too feminine. He hated ill-prepared documents and briefings, risky improvisations that might catch him off-guard. What he liked, and he always said so, was orderly thinking. But there was more to it than that; it would be unjust to reduce the wave of rationality which he let loose on the public service to the level of an intellectual fancy for organizational flow charts and diagrams. Rationality was vital for an organization which had been going off in every direction during the 1960s and which had to adapt rapidly to scientific, technical and social changes in Canada and throughout the world. When Pierre Trudeau took power, the lack of co-ordination between departments was sometimes politically embarassing for the government. "Trudeau and his advisers were determined not to continue the government-by-crisis pattern which had characterized the Diefenbaker and Pearson administrations. Trudeau had been horrified by the succession of scandals, threatened resignations, cabinet leaks and other upsets which made the Pearson minority administration a continuing exercise in improvisation by the Prime Minister. He wanted to avoid such untidy government at all costs."[6] Order was required.

The Prime Minister did two things on taking office. "When he first moved into 24 Sussex (he) hung in the stairwell, where he would see it first thing in the morning and last thing at night, a banner with a strange device: a quilt made for him by the artist Joyce Wieland, on which she patch-worked the phrase 'la Raison avant la Passion.' "[7] In the Prime Minister's Office he did even better: he installed Marc Lalonde.

Lalonde put together a top level team whose tasks were precisely defined. Everything was co-ordinated according to a strict agenda to ensure that every important decision came to the attention of the Prime Minister who had a briefing session with his staff every morning at a set time. In less than three years the staff of the Prime Minister's Office doubled.

This transformation was extended to the whole federal bureaucracy which was given to planning, centralization and staffing. So much so that the number of employees doubled within a few years. But this time, the architect was not Marc Lalonde but a young alter ego of the Prime Minister himself: Michael Pitfield.

He is relatively unknown to the public which is vaguely aware that he was one of the influential mandarins before his appointment to the Senate in 1982. And yet he left an indelible mark on the federal public service. At least that's how he was perceived by senior bureaucrats who tend to hold him personally responsible for all the ills that befell the public service and the national economy. That much is conveyed in the course of interviews and dinners where the only topic of conversation would be his privileged relationship with the Prime Minister.[8]

Admittedly, Pitfield's career is of the kind that arouses the fiercest jealousies. At twenty-nine, two years before Pierre Elliott Trudeau came to power, he was already Assistant Secretary to the Cabinet in the Privy Council Office (PCO). He became the Deputy Secretary of the Plans Division in PCO when it was established in 1969. Then he was appointed Clerk of the Council, something which was done

67

over the heads of many senior mandarins whose own background and experience would have qualified them for this post. . . and who never forgave him.

It will be rather difficult for future historians to unravel the passionate animosities he triggered, the ideas which belong to the Prime Minister, the ideas that were in the air at that time, and what Pitfield himself wanted to achieve. But, as time passes, this knowledge loses its importance. What matters is that the Prime Minister and the Clerk of the Privy Council always worked together on the same themes and ideas, and that the friendship which linked them reinforced the Prime Minister's interest in the bureaucracy and contributed to breaking down the separation between the bureaucracy and politics in Canada.

The Trudeau-Pitfield combination looked at public administration from the single perspective of rationalization. True, the models developed in the 1970s for planning, co-ordination and management, were remarkable and worthy of the interest they aroused in other parts of the world. But these models paid little or no attention to experience, expenditures and administrative life as it really exists, from employee morale to the perverse side effects which Hubert Laframboise has collectively called "the counter-management."[9] Whenever it seemed that the ideal organization would not work, the reaction was to blame the model and come up with a new one, more abstract and more brilliant than ever. . . on paper. . . and the reforms applied to the public service succeeded each other as quickly as governments in Italy.

Yet, how beautiful all those theories were!

A Decade of Enlightenment
The great rationalization of the public service rested on three concepts:
- the possibility of knowing the future and of planning government activities according to an analytical understanding of society;
- the possibility of co-ordinating all these activities in a clear and rational way;
- the need to recruit new men with new ideas to take charge.[10]

68

Planning

Planning belongs to the whole period under study, and was not the exclusive concern of the Canadian government and of its Prime Minister. The future, which had until then belonged to dreamers, prophets, fortune tellers and to the Soviet Five Year Plan, had already become the object of crucial political activity under the influence of Robert McNamara who introduced futuristic scenarios into the American Defence Department. What had originally been military strategy quickly became a social science. In Rome, the Club of the same name saw the future in terms of catastrophes and urged world governments to act accordingly. In Paris, Futuribles advised public authorities on the possibility of listing priorities according to the methods of traditional prospective analysis. In 1973, more than 300 of the greatest minds in the world gathered at an international congress in Frascati, Italy, to meditate on the future (incidentally, none of the predictions made in the course of the meeting ever came to pass). Fiat earned the admiration of its competitors by hiring some specialists to draft "the scenario of a carless world," and the Commission for Territorial Planning and Development in Paris paid a considerable sum for "a scenario of the unthinkable" which got every intellectual in Paris chattering away. Improved forecasting methods were given exotic and intriguing names such as the Delphi Method or Matrix.

Without going overboard on futurology, Pierre Trudeau had sufficient confidence in it to believe that systematic use of prospective analysis was essential for any policy that tried to deal with future trends. He firmly believed in the progress of knowledge and in political science, or rather in the use of the social sciences including economics, for political decisions.

"With this knowledge we are wide awake, alert, capable of action; no longer are we blind, inert pawns of fate,"[11] he told an enthusiastic Liberal thinkers' conference in 1969. It was in fact the modern version of Francis Bacon's saying, "Knowledge is power."

No sooner said than done. It began on a small scale and in a way that was ominous for the bureaucracy. The walls of the Privy Council

Office were covered with charts labelled in impressive jargon, "intended to capture and interrelate the government's many planning exercises" which "provided an often bizarre iconography for the corridors of power."[12] Jim Davey, programs secretary in the Prime Minister's Office, spent a number of months applying industrial engineering techniques to government systems. One of his ideas was an audio-visual reflection room.

Such an overflow of youthful enthusiasm drew smiles from old timers in the public service and from journalists as well. They talked about "the babble of dreamers,"[13] of "Athens-on-the-Rideau," and, as one anonymous wit put it, "Expo PCO." But humour turned bitter as it dawned on everyone that this wasn't the kind of harmless gadgetry that the mighty dream up for their own amusement. The Prime Minister intended not only to probe the future but to act in accordance with what he saw. He asked the Privy Council Office to set up a "Cabinet planning system" and he invited the greatest specialists of the time, such as Yehezkel Dror for consultation . The findings were applied and translated into bureaucratic terms by Michael Kirby, thirty years old with a degree in mathematics. He later described the system in these words: "In its more comprehensive form, this concern for planning was characterized by the 'systems' approach. This approach was an almost total rejection of the personalized manner of policy-making in the 1950s and early 1960s. Emphasis was placed on designing the right structure which would enable the identification of potential problems along with the development of the best policies."[14]

The idea was to use systems analysis to identify the future situation and problems of Canada at the end of the century, and to devise programs and policies that could anticipate events. In the usually transparent words of their authors, the idea was "to help ministers know what they were doing."

In the realm of theory, once the stage of reflection has been completed, the time comes for action and for drawing up priorities. This gave rise to yet another offshoot of the planning urge, the authorship of which belongs to Michael Pitfield. It became the most important Cabinet committee, dealing with Priorities and Planning, which ministers attended only on invitation, and whose ambitious functions were, at least on paper, obviously useful and impeccably logical.

Success, it was thought, depended on perfect co-ordination between departments and harmony between ministers, who would all accept that some department other than their own be designated of priority interest and who would all work together for the common good instead of their own particular interest. It constituted, as Michael Kirby expressed it, "the advent of collegiality." Cabinet committees were coming into their own.

The Advent of Collegiality

Cabinet committees were the product of hope and of logic. But they also embodied, in a way that is perhaps not so obvious, the dream of enlightened despotism which had inflamed the minds of eighteenth century philosophers. The Prime Minister, also known as the Philosopher-King, insisted on chairing meetings of ministers who, he felt, should indulge in deeper reflection. "Ministers", he explained, "tended to be their own bosses in their own sections and therefore their deputy ministers, to the same extent, tended to be their own bosses too. They didn't have to submit their policies to the countervailing forces of the cross-examination, or cross-fertilization, for all I know, of other ministers and other departments. That's the way I've been trying to make the government function, by telling a minister look, before you do something with such and such a program, you must realize the impact it will have on another department."[15]

Later on, one of his advisors confirmed, "He was on that point quite candid; he firmly believed that everyone was interested in truth and that truth would result from the discussion of several intelligent people. When he mastered his subject and thought he had it—like the constitution—he was pretty abrasive and did not let anyone talk, but when he knew little on a subject, he was humble, asked questions and let the others talk. . . and he would wait and wait and wait. . . "

Nine committees or think tanks were thus set up right at the beginning of the 1970s: Culture and Native Affairs, External Policy and Defence, Economic Policy, Social Policy, Government Operations (with a secretariat in the Operations Division of the Privy Council Office), Legislation and House Planning, Priorities and Planning, and Federal-Provincial Relations (with a secretariat run jointly by the Federal-Provincial Relations Office and the Treasury Board).

The decision-making process henceforth proceeded along a zigzag course:

o   a brief is prepared by the department and approved by the minister;
o   it goes to the Privy Council Office;
o   it is forwarded to the appropriate committee;
o   the committee drafts a report;
o   the report is forwarded to Cabinet.

The number of topics under consideration grew at such a rate that less important matters were sent back to committee for a decision. Only major issues ever made it on to the Cabinet's agenda, but they could be sent back to committee for further study.

In this back-and-forth movement of documents, some of which were several hundred pages long, the Privy Council Office was organizer, co-ordinator and transmitter, a role which one might see as purely instrumental and secretarial. However, this view seriously underestimates the consultative power which it assumed at the time. The personnel of the Privy Council exercized great responsibilities and wielded considerable influence. They were the ones who briefed the Prime Minister and the committee chairman on a memorandum, overstepping departmental experts. They were also the ones who drafted the decision in the Record of Decisions. Moreover, beginning in 1969, the Privy Council had considerable power regarding proposals for appointments of senior members in the bureaucracy who obviously would not want to do anything that might jeopardize their own careers.

While it would be ridiculous to believe that everything flowed from the Privy Council staff, its influence was considerable and all the more fearsome since it was impossible to assess, thus leaving a great deal to the imagination. In certain cases, its influence has been documented. In other cases, it was strongly suspected, thereby reinforcing the Ottawa scuttlebutt about some phantom organization even more powerful than the ministers.

But who were these shadowy people?

The Inner Sanctum

The first characteristic of these people from the shadows was their large number. According to Colin Campbell, the growth of the central control agencies speeded up after 1975 when the staff in the Prime Minister's Office had already doubled.

The second characteristic, apparently so evident that it escaped the notice of most observers, was that, until 1976, they were mostly men, transforming the central agencies into male bastions. This can be confirmed with a glance at the telephone directories for that period. When one realizes that the central control agencies were the springboard for the most successful careers in the national capital, then it becomes easy to see why women began to lag even further behind than at the time of the mandarins of the old school.

Other traits have been analysed by Colin Campbell and George Szablowski in a volume with the revealing title of The Superbureaucrats[16] which analysed the answers given to a questionnaire similar to the one which had previously been used by John Porter.[17]

The superbureaucrats were young. The average age in the central control agencies was 45 compared to 51 in the upper echelons of the public service.[18] But this is an average for all the people in these agencies and says very little about those who had been nurtured on royal jelly, the high flyers whose influence was felt in terms of power and ideas and who, in some cases, were not even 35 years old.

They had very little experience of departmental requirements or in private enterprise.[19] The prevailing ideology stressed creativity and allowed fresh ideas to compensate for inexperience. This kind of outlook was not limited to the central control agencies; it affected the whole government as well as the whole country. But it was particularly strong in the control agencies because the Prime Minister himself was personally committed to new ideas. He took great care in selecting those people from the ranks of the bureaucracy or among university graduates who would become the mandarins of tomorrow. He propelled

73

them to the summit of the hierarchy, over the heads of older mandarins who had been anticipating their own promotion and who saw in the whole process the unholy intrusion of politics into public administration.

The young superbureaucrats had graduated in political science and economics. According to Campbell and Szablowski, "91 per cent of our respondents have at least a Bachelor degree, an 11 per cent increase over Chartrand and Pond's[20] figure covering senior officials in all departments."[21] One interesting fact, which belies the Toronto rumour about the domination of "french power" in Ottawa, is that none of the front line players, with very few exceptions, were francophone university graduates.

The young superbureaucrats also had their own jargon which differed from the traditional bureaucratic one, ponderous and full of redundancies designed for sticking as closely as possible to regulations. What they spoke and wrote was a sort of academic jargon, daring but often hollow, which allowed them to communicate directly with their counterparts in the private sector who had been schooled in the same manner.[22]

They were careerists. The classical school of sociology and Max Weber have described the bureaucratic ethic in terms of a duty whose reward is a sense of accomplishment. In a sense, the mandarins of the postwar period appeared to have been moulded according to Weber's model, but the young superbureaucrats were different, and possibly, more sincere.

"The largest percentage of them said they entered the public service for reasons which related more to career success and management skills in general than bureaucratic service in particular. Some 60 per cent pointed out that they came to government because they could not find a satisfactory position in the private sector or were unhappy with the one they had."[23] Another important fact was that career paths in the central agencies were no longer influenced by the bureaucratic old boys' club which until then had had a stranglehold on the admission of young recruits. The young superbureaucrats had direct access to the Prime Minister and some of them saw him even more often than members of the Cabinet. To attract the Prime Minister's notice was the dream of a great many empire-builders of the day.

The competition went far beyond the simple pleasures of office politics. The age, mode of selection, the mentality, and particularly the mobility of the superbureaucrats created demands and expectations which reverberated throughout the Ottawa bureaucracy. The unusual flexibility of the selection process stimulated many ambitions which were not kept in check by the traditional brakes of seniority and experience. At the same time the selection process stimulated competition among a group which demographically was already highly competitive. "By the nature of the process, you have to promote yourself. The first guy on high ground wins the day. You have to get in and fight," confessed one of the superbureaucrats.[24] The game itself became more interesting than the actual stakes—the programs—and power was pursued for its own sake, a situation which Doug Hartle has so well described: "One reason a great many senior servants stay in Ottawa, even when they could move elsewhere, is the fascination of the play of power—even as a voyeur. It's an endless poker game with in some cases enormous stakes."[25]

Rational Follies

Everything was in place. The Canadian government could now apply itself to shaping a golden future. It could put its own ideas in order and those of the bureaucracy which had developed without a central brain during the preceding decade. Everything was in place except an awareness of the limits of a rational approach. Everything was in place except for a profound knowledge of bureaucratic culture. Everything was in place except the will to make the best possible use of the enormous resources vested in the 200,000 employees which the Prime Minister had inherited in 1968. During the 1970s, the octopus of government expanded its reach. The federal service grew by 25 per cent and eventually lost touch with its own employees.

The Tentacles of the State

Reason, which many people believe to be dispassionate, is in fact enthusiastic because it knows no bounds. Intellectual exploration in general and in the economic and social sciences in particular, deals with the discovery of increasingly complex and numerous interrelations between a wide range of facts or among economic and social variables. Towards the end of the 1960s, on university campuses, this took the form of interdisciplinary committees who discovered that the principal branches of knowledge (philosophy, sociology, psychology, urban planning, biology, etc.) overlapped on many points, leading them to create new academic disciplines based on their interaction (socio-pedagogy, social psychoanalysis, psychosociology, urban sociology, etc.).

The trend was duplicated in government. The committees where ministers and their advisors met were also interdisciplinary, and during the discussions participants discovered new realms which the government had to control if it was to govern efficiently. To promote industrial development in a given region, it became necessary to control foreign investment, urbanization and the environment. To assist agriculture, it became necessary to regulate even more tightly certain sectors of the economy such as transportation. Contrary to what many people thought, these policies were not inspired by a Marxist desire to control all exchanges within Canadian society, but simply by a desire to maximize government intervention, making use of the best resources and the best data available. It would be unjust to criticize those who had the responsibility of government for wanting to be as open-minded as possible concerning the consequences of their policies. In principle, they were right.

Moreover, Canadians themselves contributed to this process by their increasing insistence that the government become the chosen instrument for the correction of social and economic disparities.

The temptation of the leviathan therefore became irresistible. Ideas took shape in the government and the public service grew accordingly.

Expansion took three distinct forms. First of all, it continued the traditions established during the preceding period. New programs and new areas of intervention were mapped out within the framework of existing departments (Communications; Consumer and Corporate Affairs; Energy, Mines and Resources; Environment; Industry and Foreign Trade; Manpower and Immigration). Junior departments were also appended to existing ones (Multiculturalism, Fisheries, Fitness and Amateur Sport, Small Business, and the Canadian International Development Agency). Agencies and councils such as the Art Bank were also set up to deal with specific problems. It was a great period for what J.E. Hodgetts called "spill-over." As he wrote: "The extent of the growth and proliferation of government-owned and government-controlled agencies was starkly revealed before the Public Accounts Committee in 1977 when Treasury Board officials reported that there were several hundred agencies in existence at that time. (The Financial Administration Act listed only fifty-four agencies in its schedule)."[26]

In other cases, this new expansion was more like an outgrowth in that it was related to the co-ordination and the administration of the whole service. It took several forms. The power and the staff of the central control agencies took another leap forward. Three new agencies were also established: the Federal-Provincial Relations Office in 1974, the Ministry of State for Social Development and the Ministry of State for Economic and Regional Development in 1979, which were all outgrowths of sections of the Privy Council Office, too small for their ambitions. Co-ordinating ministries were also organized at the limit of the control agencies, such as Urban Affairs and Science and Technology. "Without substantial programs of their own to administer, these Ministries were given the task of achieving their objectives by influencing and co-ordinating the activities of other agencies."[27]

The rationalization of decision-making processes reverberated throughout the public service, reproducing the same effect from department to department, from division to division, from one unit to another, like so many Russian dolls that fit snugly into each other. The reform of Cabinet committees required the establishment in each department of a special section able to meet planning requirements. The system for spending accountability was so complex and unreliable that it seemed necessary to establish new control mechanisms. The post of Comptroller General was established in 1976.

Then, because of the general expansion of the public service, it became necessary to deal with the problem of personnel management.

Between 1969 and 1976, the public service grew by 37 per cent, the number of employees rising from 199,720 to 273,167. This brought about such major structural changes that their magnitude is still difficult to grasp.

One of the major consequences was the unbelievable volatility of the public service, which can be seen in Table 9.

Table 9: Appointments to the Public Service and Within the Public Service, 1970-1976

	Appointments to the P.S.	Appointments within the P.S.	Total
1970	23,055	30,279	53,334
1971	27,706	38,969	66,675
1972	38,568	49,916	88,484
1973	38,979	59,536	98,515
1974	46,567	78,232	124,799
1975	36,251	90,920	127,171
1976	30,201	91,031	121,232
Total	241,327	438,883	680,210

Source: Public Service Commission, Annual Reports, 1970 to 1976.

During a period of six years, the Public Service Commission proceeded with close to 700,000 staffing activities, replacing those who left in great numbers (205,220 between 1970 and 1976), appointing new ones, transferring and mainly promoting old ones with the rhythm of a fast waltz.

And so here we are, in 1976, with 270,000 public servants literally always on the move, some of them moving so rapidly that no one was ever able to judge the quality of their performance.

There was a price to pay: an increasingly pronounced structural imbalance. Ironically, the wave of rationalization which was sweeping public administration stopped at its very door: no one realized the extraordinary changes that resulted, affecting its life and its business. Everyone was too concerned with moving ahead to stop and consider internal management, an area which tends to be neglected by thinkers great and small.   Yet the first symptoms of a bureaucratic malaise were already visible for those who wanted to look (but who thinks of health in the midst of a feast)?

First Symptoms
The Great Structural Imbalances
No one really knows what equilibrium in public administration means, any more than one knows what mental equilibrium means, where it begins and where it ends. In private enterprise, the consensus is that an organization is healthy when production goes smoothly, when it seems this will continue for some time, and when employee morale is satisfactory as measured by signs such as the rates of absenteeism, alcoholism, turnover, or vandalism.

Regarding the public service, any debate on the problem of internal equilibrium would likely lead to the establishment of yet another control agency. In truth, there is no model and no product. And there has never been any systematic enquiry into employee morale, no doubt out of a desire not to know. Since such an enquiry would affect a quarter of a million people, it would amount to a study of Canadian society as a whole. And what does equilibrium mean for Canadians?

It might be argued that the steady growth of the deficit is proof of something gone wrong in the organization, but one might also argue that it is only a symptom, not conclusive evidence. Expenditures are really political decisions, and it is possible to spend madly and wildly in an organization that runs perfectly and without a hitch.

Nevertheless, without going into a comprehensive health examination, it is possible to point to five structural imbalances which had already appeared in 1975 and which became more pronounced with time.

Instability
Throughout the 1970s, government employees played musical chairs. Rapid change associated with abrupt growth encouraged personnel to seek their fortune wherever it seemed most favourable, and, it was apparent that certain growth sectors ensured rapid career advancement.

The general movement was really launched at the Cabinet level. During a period of ten years, the Communications Department had seven different ministers, followed by Industry and International Trade which had six. And whenever there is a new minister, there is generally a new deputy minister, and some new associate deputy ministers as well. During this period it was not rare to see a complete staff follow its general on the move, with the record in this respect no doubt being held by Lloyd Axworthy who seemed to favour massive migrations from one department to another.

The turnover of deputy ministers was just as impressive as that of the ministers. The Lambert Commission report pointed out that the rate of turnover between 1974 and 1978 was double that for the period 1959-1964. But this was not a situation peculiar to Ottawa. The provincial service in Quebec also had its musical chairs. "As many deputy ministers were appointed between 1960 and 1978, as from 1867 to 1960," lamented Roch Bolduc.[28]

There was a similar trend in the upper echelons of the federal service. Promotions and transfers doubled between 1968 and 1972.

Such a high rate of turnover had major consequences for the life and outlook of the organization. Some federal employees never had the time to become familiar with their responsibilities within a department and to benefit from the kind of knowledge that only experience provides. If one considers that a large number of people at the top of the hierarchy were younger than forty and were mostly inexperienced on entering the public service, then it is easy to realize how disastrous the results could have been in many instances.

Employee morale, as described in the Lambert report was profoundly affected by all these people waltzing from job to job:

> Frequent change in the leadership of departments, by breaking management continuity, can undermine the morale of organizations. Moreover, claims cannot be made that wide experience helps make up for the high mobility of deputies. Nearly 80 per cent of present deputies received their initial appointments as deputy heads since 1971, and about half have neither worked at lower levels in the department they administer, nor had the benefit of significant similar experience in related fields before joining the federal government. . . . Departmental managers have experienced too often the pattern of events that follows

replacement of the deputy head. A new deputy means re-orientation, a decision-making pause, potential new priorities, possible re-organization, new relationships, and the anxiety that can precede the establishment of the basic trust upon which all successful organizations depend.[29]

It must also be pointed out that during this whole period of musical chairs when young men were propelled to the top levels of the hierarchy, the morale of women with university degrees fell to its lowest level ever. They were very often denied access to the best jobs because supposedly "they did not have managerial experience."

Even if a high turnover accelerates career advancement, it is still a very threatening situation for those who are already at the top. It breeds insecurity and diverts energies which would otherwise be expended on administrative tasks. It encourages competition and makes "production" a means of attaining personal goals. Moreover, since most of this movement accompanied promotions, many stable managers gradually got the idea that immobility was a sign of failure. This only contributed to deepen the general restlessness. And so Ottawa carried on with its golden triangles (the central control agencies), its slogans (location, location, location), its greed (always more) and its plush residential districts (deputy minister).

High turnover encourages irresponsibility in that those who initiate programs and ideas are seldom there to reap what they have sowed. The point was made by Doug Hartle: "I was always impressed by the fine sense of timing displayed by many public servants. They seemed to have an uncanny instinct of when it is time to move. Having initiated some grandiose project in a department, they know exactly when to move along before they can be held accountable for less than promised results. In this way they can, by a series of astute moves, appear to be innovative and energetic while their successors are perceived to be incompetent."[30]

Ottawa versus the Regions

The equilibrium between headquarters and branch offices is always a sensitive issue in large organizations. Too small a staff at headquarters runs the risk of not being able to govern; too large a staff risks antagonizing the branch offices and communications become increasingly difficult.

Available evidence shows that the point of equilibrium, which Canadian regionalism makes somewhat precarious, has never really preoccupied the promoters of growth. As a result, Ottawa-Hull expanded when compared to the regions, as shown in Table 10.

Table 10: Percentage of Personnel Located in Ottawa-Hull Compared to the Regions

Year	Percentage
1970	24.9
1975	27.2

Source: Public Service Commission, Annual Reports, 1970 and 1975.

Growth was differentiated in the sense that the largest increases were registered for the top levels of the public service in Ottawa-Hull. As shown in Table 11, 70 per cent of top level civil servants during that period were located in the national capital.

Table 11: Senior Managers by Regions, 1976

Region	Number
Alberta	224
British Columbia	302
Manitoba	217
National Capital Region	6,054
New Brunswick	121
Newfoundland	68
North-West Territories	18
Nova Scotia	240
Ontario	631
Prince Edward Island	12
Quebec	511
Saskatchewan	113
Yukon	14
Abroad	123
Total	8,648

Source: Public Service Commission, unpublished data.

Many factors explain the imbalance between the national capital and the regions. The first one is obviously political: the Trudeau government was a strong believer in centralization and showed it on numerous occasions. But the imbalance is also the result of bureaucratic expansion. According to an interim report written for the Federal-Provincial Relations Office in 1977, "A major side effect of this expansion has been to accentuate rivalries in federal-provincial relations, especially those between Quebec and the federal government."[31]

But there is more to it than that. Agencies and departments responsible for control and co-ordination proliferated at that time. They set up shop in Ottawa and they required a very large number of senior executives.

Federal public servants located in the provinces took on an air of poor relations; those who were asked to move there thought of it as an exile.

Obviously, this overrepresentation coupled with the prosperity of Ottawa did nothing to counteract the growing alienation between the federal government and the rest of the country. Resentment had something solid to stand on: in 1970, a metropolitan census showed that Ottawa-Hull topped the list for income per family with $28,290.

Chiefs and Indians

The growth of the public service was not uniform; in Ottawa-Hull it took place in the middle and top levels of the hierarchy. The following tables show a situation which gets worse as the years go by, something that will be discussed in the next chapter.

To be precise, one would have to say that the rush towards the top was essentially a masculine phenomenon whose real nature was not apparent because of the large number of women hired in non-management jobs. When these two separate groups are merged, the reassuring result is a hierarchical pyramid with a wide base, as the following table shows.

Table 12: Federal Public Service, National Capital, by Hierarchical Levels, 1976

	Numbers	Percentages
Upper Management	6,054	9.5
Middle Management	12,439	19.5
Officers	16,684	26.1
Support	28,606	44.8
Total	63,783	100.0

Source: Public Service Commission, unpublished data.

However, when the data is broken down on the basis of sex, the pyramid for women becomes very wide at the base, while in the case of men it acquires an onion-shaped structure, as in the following table.

Table 13: Male Employees in the Federal Public Service, National Capital, by Hierarchical Levels, 1976

	Numbers	Percentages
Upper Management	5,749	15.3
Middle Management	10,790	28.6
Officers	11,304	30.0
Support	9,813	26.1
Total	37,656	100.0

Source: Public Service Commission, unpublished data.

In other words, in 1976, nearly 44 per cent of the men in the National Capital Region had reached at least middle management level. But this is nothing compared to the 55 per cent who would be at that level in 1984.

But this generalization is not applicable to all departments. Some of the operational ones such as Public Works and Transport, retained a classical pyramidal structure with a wide base, while others went beyond the onion and reached even more exotic shapes.

In some cases, such as the Privy Council Office, the hierarchical pyramid took the form of a bulbous mushroom.

Table 14: Male Employees, Privy Council Office, by Hierarchical Levels, 1976

Upper Management	39
Middle Management	13
Officers	15
Support	49
Total	116

Source: Public Service Commission, unpublished data.

In other cases, such as the Treasury Board, the pyramidal structure was totally inverted and looked like a strawberry, to continue with these edible metaphors.

Table 15: Male Employees, Treasury Board, by Hierarchical Levels, 1976

Upper Management	271
Middle Management	84
Officers	63
Support	27
Total	445

Source: Public Service Commission, unpublished data.

The profusion of high level public service jobs in the national capital can be explained in several ways.   During the 1960s it was necessary to attract and retain university graduates who might have been tempted by the greener pastures of private enterprise.   A large proportion of employees in the national capital region had university degrees.

The prevailing ideology at the time was decidedly expansionist. This phenomenon had started in the universities where the practice was to inflate student grades to such an extent that their expectations and performance were dissociated from the reality of the previous generation.   One again, Doug Hartle, one of the frankest observers of that period, recalls: "To my dying day, I'll never forget the creation of the Department of the Environment. It was started from scratch—a collection of bits and pieces from Fisheries, Energy, Mines and Resources, Transport and what have you with about 150 people in the SX category. Within three weeks there was a request for another 155 or so. I fought this for two years. I was hauled before ministers and castigated for holding up the government's environmental policy. Eventually the actual increase was substantially smaller. I think I earned my keep on that one. . . . But God, the fighting that went on was beyond belief."[32] Finally, the whole system of comparative self-evaluation collapsed and the ensuing escalation engendered "dissatisfaction by comparison."

Men and Women

Women were the biggest losers in the two periods of public service expansion. During the first one, they were automatically eliminated by the preference clause applicable to war veterans. The 1950s were no better because of the context of that period: as we have seen, the public service acquired a paramilitary structure within which the large number of veterans imposed an ideology which was hardly inclined to feminism. Women were simply "the girls", as the Civil Service Commission annual reports referred to them.

Anything might have been possible during the second wave of expansion which completely rejected the values of the first one. Anything might have been possible all the more so because there was at that time a large supply of women with university degrees. In 1970 they accounted for 30 per cent of all university graduates. But nothing happened, or almost nothing. On this matter the Pearson and Trudeau governments did not show the same openness of mind that they had displayed with respect to bilingualism. Moreover, at a time when it was necessary to be pushy, that is, towards the end of the sixties and the beginning of the seventies, burgeoning feminism was not strong enough politically to be a persuasive instrument of pressure, even if women were starting to invade the labour market.

Therefore, the great recruiting wave of the 1960s and 1970s left women behind, or did not keep them (this is a plausible

86

hypothesis. . . but a wrong one according to those who were there at the time).

Worse, while more women born between 1940 and 1950 had university degrees than those born between 1925 and 1930, they were more poorly represented in the ranks of the public service. In 1984, women born between 1925 and 1930 represented 12 per cent of people with degrees in mathematics and statistics in that age group in the public service; but those born between 1940 and 1945 made up only 7 per cent of those with degrees in this discipline within that particular age group. They make up 5.5 per cent of economics graduates born between 1930 and 1935 and only 3.8 per cent of those born between 1945 and 1950.

The result, according to one observer, was a categorical "rejection, so unconscious that men are sincerely offended when one tries to make them understand." Table 16 tells the story. In 1976 almost half of the male employees in the public service had reached management level, while more than nine-tenths of female employees were in non-managerial jobs.

Table 16: Federal Employees, National Capital Region, 1976, by Hierarchical Levels and by Sex

	Men	Percentages	Women	Percentages
Upper Management	5,749	15.2	305	1.2
Middle Managment	10,790	28.6	1,649	6.3
Officers	11,304	30.0	5,380	20.6
Support	9,813	26.1	18,792	71.9
Total	37,656		26,126	

Source: Public Service Commission, unpublished data.

Age

A large proportion of decision-makers who quickly reached the top of their category were younger than 45, as shown in Table 17. For 25 years they partly blocked the advancement possibilities of the generation following theirs.

Table 17: Employees under 45 at the Top of their Category at the End of 1976, in Percentages.

Group	Percentage
FI 7	48.4
AS 8	23.7
PM 7	36.0
PE 7	26.9
SX 3	30.8
ES 5	38.3

Source: Nicole S. Morgan, Charles Moubarak, "Nowhere to Go?", Montreal, Institute for Research on Public Policy, 1981.

The First Signs of Anxiety

In 1975, the bureaucracy was still unconcerned. Like all structural problems, current ones were visible only to those who cared to have a look at the foundations. Few took the trouble. 1975 was a remarkably good year for everyone, even if the euphoria of the 1960s had cooled a bit. Optimism persisted among the bureaucrats in the national capital.

Yet dark clouds had been gathering over the political landscape. Inflation seemed uncontrollable, and it was a worrisome problem for Canadians and Cabinet ministers with little interest in the abstract and long range plans put forward by the bureaucracy of the central agencies in government. Many of them did not take kindly to the influence exerted on the Prime Minister by Michael Pitfield and his colleagues. They accused them of cutting him off from the political and social reality of the country. Some ministers, we might add, did not take kindly to being relegated to second rank behind those who evidently had direct access to the Prime Minister.

In 1972, when he was returned to office heading a minority government, Pierre Trudeau found that he could no longer ignore his ministers. He sent Pitfield into exile as deputy minister of Consumer and Corporate Affairs. For a while, the personnel of the central agencies were more discreet, but the rest of the bureaucracy continued as if nothing had happened.

It was only in 1975 and 1976, as inflation continued to gain ground, that things really started to go wrong. A decision was made to cut back spending and to impose a wage and price freeze.

At the government level, this resulted in the establishment of the Anti-Inflation Board and the symbolic layoff of a few hundred employees. A limit of 1.5 per cent was imposed on the growth of the public service and salaries of executives and deputy ministers were frozen for one year. This provoked a sixth imbalance. With salaries being blocked at the top, but not at the middle of the pyramid, the inevitable happened: the salaries of a number of subordinate employees caught up with and even surpassed those of their superiors.

But this was a minor detail, since the freeze on mandarins' salaries was only a demagogic gesture. There was worse to come. In March 1976, the Auditor General, James Macdonnell, gained political stardom with his famous quote, already cited in the Introduction, concerning the Government's lack of control over expenditures. In his report, he "mounted a major offensive against abuses and deficiencies in financial practices, which he found to be 'significantly below acceptable standards of quality and effectiveness.' "[33]

Ottawa began to wake up. The criticism of the Auditor General had such an impact that the government announced a Royal Commission on Financial Management and Accountability and a task force to look into the administration of the merit principle in the public service.

However, things had gone too far for such innocuous moves to have any effect at all. The public service, like any large organization, takes a while to adjust to a new situation. But when it does so at last, its resistance to change is so great that any reform becomes impossible, even if deemed urgent. By 1975, the public service was hooked on growth as if it were a drug; any pressure to the contrary was manipulated by the system so as to be neutralized. Hugh Hanson, former assistant deputy minister for Urban Affairs, recalls, "I remember that just before the 1974 election there was a big flap on that Cabinet would impose a freeze on the civil service. We got directives to fill all vacancies, and were told that the PSC would expedite fast hiring. This was a conscious, deliberate thwarting by the public service of the expected political will."[34] The same kind of panic took place in 1981, just before the announcement of the so-called 6 and 5, when rumour in Ottawa had it that a staffing freeze was in the making.

Problems snowballed on their own momentum. The feeling was, no doubt, that it would be easier to let matters drift in the hope that they would eventually stabilize than to make the effort of correcting them. Economic studies with ominous conclusions piled up on ministers' desks without ever being published. "Why would a minister release them? It's like asking a man to beat himself with his own stick," joked a former deputy minister.

So the government gave up on economic management. The members of the royal commission and the task force were thanked for their excellent work which was given the same fate as most studies on the public service. The recommendations were shelved.

In 1977, the Public Service Commission announced that the number of government employees had reached a record 283,000. And then, according to Statistics Canada, there were 330,000 government employees under the heading of general government, and another 144,000 in public enterprises.

In Ottawa, everyday life went on undisturbed even under a darkening sky. But many chickens would soon be coming home to roost.

4: THE RETURN OF PASSION

The Expert in Politics

The public service continued on its erratic path, its irrationality aggravated by the decision-making procedures that had been installed. This was the great irony of reason applied to public administration: it encouraged all kinds of follies because it had neglected the most important element in any organization, the human one. Not the element that humanizes but the one that explains motivations and leads to a very simple question: what causes an individual or a group of decision-makers, political or administrative or any employee to agree to:

o   work together even though their interests may differ;

o   accept the idea of productivity modeled on the private sector but without a marketable product and the risk of bankruptcy;

o   recognize the common good in spite of contradictory objectives.

This type of oversight is not limited to the public sector. The American bestseller, In Search of Excellence, is a stinging criticism of large corporations which, in the 1960s believed in a direct relationship between rationality and production when there was no problem in putting anything on the market. It was only with the recession that corporate managers became aware that abstract procedures did not necessarily work and that one might have to come back to such outmoded but explosive notions as charisma, emotional motivations and a sense of belonging.[1]

It was the kind of oversight which is part and parcel of contemporary culture with its enthusiastic faith in the new administrative, organizational and pedagogical sciences, and with its refusal to have a close look at values and at qualitative individual differences. Reliance was placed on the kind of dichotomy which says: individuals are good and intrinsically self-motivated while the system, the organization, the structures are all bad and must be transformed.

This was also a cyclical oversight, a minor variant of the struggle which compares technical men, in Weber's sense of the word, to the Machiavellis of history. Unquestionably, the Trudeau era was one not of idealism—the word would be too strong—but of structuralism, an era of faith in the absolute power of process, to the detriment of what the Prince had learned at his mother's knee: "No donkey has ever walked without a stick and a carrot."

This oversight had incalculable consequences for the public service. In this void, there prospered an organization whose true sense was lost to those who worked within it, who used it, and governed it. Reason had finally come up against passion.

Wheeling and Dealing
All too Human
The first clash between reason and passion took place in Cabinet and in the decision-making process. Recent reforms had aimed at planning, co-ordinating and facilitating the activities of individual ministers and at providing them with opportunities to discuss ideas, something which they could never do by themselves because of an unusually heavy burden of work. This was vital because of the growing complexity of government. In fact, many fruitful discussions took place at these meetings. But these exchanges generated so much extra work, so many conflicts, and so many compromises, that the ultimate objectives were lost in the shuffle. Ministers were bureaucratized while their advisers

were politicized. Tensions rose and the common good simply became the expression of the lowest common denominator.

Overwork or Delegated Authority

The overwork generated by the Cabinet committee system began to take its toll immediately. Each committee generally met once a week and was attended by a dozen ministers, each of whom belonged to at least three committees. Attendance ate up between twelve and fifteen hours a week, to which must be added regular Cabinet meetings and the hours needed to scan the endless stream of papers drafted by the Privy Council Office.

As a result, ministers had little time for visiting their constituencies. They cut themselves off from the various regions of the country which were experiencing pronounced alienation from the central government. This was the time of agitation in Quebec and of rebellion in the West. It was also the time when "popular sentiment shifted away from support for big government."[2]

Ministers transformed themselves into readers of ponderous theses where initiative must always give way to compromise. "Innovative ideas still emerge from the civil service, but the process of decision-making at the Cabinet level is so complex nowadays that individual contributions are quickly submerged in a deluge of documentation," lamented Mitchell Sharp, who added that he could "not imagine ministers of St-Laurent's day agreeing to read the numerous and voluminous papers we were presented with from week to week."[3] Collegiality was nothing but waiting one's turn on Cabinet committee schedules.

Ministers were playing hooky. "As a result, committee attendance in many instances was very low... (and) the volume of cabinet documentation prepared for consideration in Committee often went unread except by the minister responsible and keenly interested colleagues," according to A. Doerr.[4]

There was little choice but to delegate deputy ministers and assistant deputy ministers to sit on committees. The ministers also had to take Privy Council documents increasingly on trust, for lack of time. According to Robert Andras, there was no Machiavellianism involved:

"The problem is that in that impossible job, in which you spend your days submerged in paper, it becomes progressively easier and easier to reach out to the familiar, to your aides and civil servants, who speak the same kind of decision-making language as you, and who you know that when you say 'give me a paper on such and such,' will produce the kind of paper that meets your decision-making needs. As a result, you reach out less and less to the unfamiliar, to the real outside world, to people."[5] The effect of collegiality was not so much to bring ministers closer to their colleagues but to their own staff.

The dividing line between politics and public administration became fuzzier than ever. To this must be added an important consideration, which was also another source of confusion. The top executives of the public service became accessible not only to their own ministers and other mandarins, but to every minister including the Prime Minister. Allegiance and loyalty towards a single minister suffered: only a saint can resist the temptation to leave a sinking ship (a minister who has come under a cloud) and try to ingratiate himself to a more favoured captain.

Rising Stress

Collegiality was not to every minister's taste. Many felt their authority being undermined. The system worked in such a way that they had to negotiate not only with their colleagues but also with these political newcomers, the bureaucrats of the central agencies. The responsibility of the bureaucrats was to keep ministers informed and to stimulate their thought processes by putting forward various policy alternatives and their consequences. Here was another irresistible temptation, as Peter Foster points out: "It would be a strange public servant who did not make his own preferred alternative appear the most attractive. Those who analyse a situation and reduce it to manageable proportions are effectively making the decision. That is not automatically to imply that the resulting decisions are bad; just to acknowledge that in modern government, the memorandum is the message."[6] Interpretation with the best of intentions is an age-old reflex: the monks of the Middle Ages who copied and recopied the works of Plato and Aristotle inserted, in addition to various embellishments, some rather suspect references to angels in the celestial realm of Ideas, to the apostles and to the Virgin Mary.

The Prime Minister also contributed to the general confusion. He was not a politician and he obviously preferred the advice of his bureaucrats to that of his ministers. In the words of one observer, until the end of the 1970s, "one had the impression that there were two cabinets: one purely for form which voters saw, and the other for substance which belonged to Michael Pitfield. The majority of ministers were quite rightly jealous of him, and they felt downgraded to the level of straw men, despised by the intellectuals who staffed the central agencies and who, thanks to the Prime Minister, were on a kind of trip that no hallucinogenic plant can provide."

The Smallest Common Denominator

Cabinet ministers were like ham in a sandwich. They were caught between the necessity of discussing the affairs of their own departments with their colleagues and that of keeping an eye on the influential members of the central agencies who had the power, even more so than any political agency, to bring to naught the best or worst conceived projects.

In these circumstances, the quest for the common good led by a group of rational ministers, assisted by their advisers committed to the truth, turned out to be more or less a joke. It wasn't that all these people were indifferent to the public interest. It was that the decision-making process gave more importance to the fantastic chess game of power relationships than to the ultimate objectives everyone had in mind. What we had here was the dynamic organizational principle: "the time spent on office politics increases with the number of players."

It also happened that the modern version of the public good, which is the choice of priorities, was just as thorny as the old one, in spite of all the newfangled techniques. The priorities, often established in great haste, were not very successful in meeting the test of time and were transformed in the light of various electoral requirements. With the advent of minority government between 1972 and 1974, long range planning gave way to more mundane concerns: staying in power.[7]

And the ministers failed to play according to the rules. An

95

independent consultant hired by the Privy Council concluded his report in these terms: "Alliances are made and log rolling becomes an inherent part of the decision-making process. I will support your program A if you'll support my program B."[8] Indeed, with the committees, ministers learned not to reason better but to bargain better. Language, or rather the manner in which words were used, became the law. Once again, the game of power took over from the purpose of power. The result reinforced the expansionist attitude which prompts any minister eager to barter to hang on to as many programs as he can, in the spirit of the old saying, "An old program is a good program."

"Only a fool would give up his pawns in a game of chess. He knows that pawns are not that valuable, that one can lose them without losing the game. But they have considerable importance in that they help deflect fatal blows or to prepare others. No minister with any judgment at all could afford to play the game of austerity and cut his department to the bone: it's like going to battle unarmed. Only the status quo or expansion will allow him to survive," one observer explained.

Canadians did not stay neutral in this game of chess: as any politician knows, it is easier to launch new programs than to cut old ones, even if the program doesn't make sense at the beginning or is lost as a result of economic or social changes. Whenever programs are threatened with cuts, voters, politicians and bureaucrats are all united by self-interest. The first ones want to keep their benefits, the second want the public's good will, and the third want to keep their jobs. As Doug Hartle jokingly said, "One might as well practise dental surgery on a shark without anaesthetic."[9]

So what we have is a disparate group of politicians and managers at the top of the federal bureaucracy, who all have the best interests of the country at heart and who must all work together to achieve it, that is, accept compromises. This division affects the decision-making process in a number of important ways.

Responsibilities tend to be diluted in a bureaucratic Cabinet. The accountability of individuals becomes the accountability of the system.

The Prime Minister's powers are enhanced since the search for consensus leads the ministers to be sensitive ultimately and even initially to the Prime Minister's views. Finally, the era of ministers who were masters of their own ship came to an end. The "prima donnas" disappeared,[10] according to Paul Pross. The big mouths in the Cabinet went out and were replaced by quiet diplomatic types. It had to be because there were now too many hands on deck: the departments had lost their ministers. Only government was left.

Illusory Decision-Making

A bureaucratic misconception gave rise to the second clash of reason and passion. It was thought that the decision-making process would rest with a team made up of bureaucrats and politicians, and operate in the style of private enterprise. They shared the same vocabulary: decision-making, collegiality, and accountability. They shared the same methods: cost-benefit analysis, management by objectives, and planning. These concepts borrowed from the world of business helped perpetuate the idea that bureaucracy and private enterprise conformed to the same dynamic laws, the only difference was that the product was not quite the same: consumer goods or services for the private sector, the common good or a program for the public sector. This confusion was in the spirit of the times. It allowed government employees to cast off the stigma of the "obedient servant", and it allowed the private sector to pass judgment on public servants in the light of its own standards.

Nothing is a greater source of confusion than this comparison between managers in the public sector and in the private sector. The reason is that interests and motivations are too widely divergent. Managers in the private sector are united behind an identical product which will make or break them. This does not mean, of course, that they work in a climate of serenity and enlightened co-operation. To think so would show ignorance of the everyday life of large corporations where feuding barons and flattery and empires are not that different today from the princely courts of the 18th century. The point is that a minimum degree of co-operation must exist because everyone is in the same boat and because rising sales satisfy everybody even if the one responsible for success happens to be detestable.

In the bureaucratic world, one must immediately understand and accept that the interests of politicians and senior bureaucrats do not necessarily coincide. Problems of conscience, to borrow an expression and a theme from Hubert Laframboise, are not unknown among those who, in addition to being bureaucrats, also happen to be Canadians, taxpayers, and involved in a variety of special interest groups.

For others also, doubts can assume a political character (in the sense of belonging to another party), although this aspect of the problem seems more hypothetical than conforming to the reality of the seventies.

Obviously, Canada never was close to the spirit of Eastern European bureaucracies where party membership is an essential condition for career advancement. However, according to a great many observers of the end of the Trudeau era, the flirt between politics and bureaucracy had become outrageous: the Canadian Unity Information Office was only the visible tip of an iceberg whose proportions no one in Ottawa wanted to measure.

However, in all honesty, it must be recognized that active and open politicization affected only part of the bureaucracy, the one whose fidelity rested on opportunism rather than idealism. "The most telling evidence", an observer said, "is the speed with which some of them became turncoats in September 1984. God, they hinted that they had been Tories all their lives. It was sickening." But again, the existence of such a group is inevitable. The rest, the majority, served a government; they could not refrain from thinking and from passing judgment.

At the beginning of the 1980s, judgment became more critical down in the boiler rooms of the ship of state, but little transpired. Friction was particularly acute in economic matters which had become the obsession of the late 1970s and early 1980s. Politicians do not mind spending when their re-election is at stake, an event they tend to identify with the public good. But this does not necessarily suit the bureaucrats who must cope with the budget cuts that will compensate for electoral expenditures.

Once more, comparison with the domestic world presents itself. There are too many similarities between public administration and a household where the domestics are asked to go easy on the silver polish while their masters are out on a spending spree buying more silver. Obviously, the domestics won't tell their masters to stop being so extravagant. And it is out of the question for senior bureaucrats to stand against the desire of politicians to ensure their re-election and not to lose face with the public. The Draft Memorandum to Cabinet,[11] a fictional story, brilliantly illustrates the uncomfortable situation of a public servant who is guilty by association of acts of pure vanity and immeasurable folly.

The story is a simple one. In order to ensure his re-election, a minister made a spending commitment without consulting the Cabinet or his colleague from Finance who refused to let it go through. A senior civil servant had to find a solution that would allow his minister to save face and at the same time appear perfectly justified in the spending estimates and in conformity with various control procedures.

These accounts are not from bitter and isolated observers. Examples are so numerous that the Auditor General himself mentions this problem in a preliminary report.

Obviously, this is far removed from the team spirit of the general staff of a private firm, although it would be naive to think that such incidents never take place in the hard-nosed world of profit-making. Let us just say that human vanity is kept in check more effectively by the realities of the market place and by colleagues whose interests are not served by promoting bankruptcy, than by politics where until now bankruptcy has seemed impossible.

In other words, public administration is partly political and is therefore not comparable to private enterprise. This is the stumbling block of rationality in the public service, and will remain so no matter how sophisticated management techniques and methods become, and whatever role is assigned to planning, control and assessment. If a decision is faulty, its execution will be so as well.

At the outset of the 1970s, the Cabinet was turning its back on the clarity of rational priorities and planning, and reverting to the concrete world of election promises and political backscratching. And the bureaucracy followed suit: calculating, evaluating, programming, rationalizing, confirming, systematizing, nodding approvingly at the emperor's new clothes. Sometimes the organization went into high gear to justify a policy which, as the rank and file knew, made little sense (the approval given to six pay-TV companies), to work out a project which had little chance of ever seeing the light of day (Pickering Airport), to work out publicity for a product which was known to be harmful (urea-formaldehyde insulating foam), or to announce ill-conceived schemes (Mirabel Airport).

Such misadventures also happen in the private sector where they are simply referred to as "mistakes." They can cost people their jobs, and they can be as frustrating as bureaucratic misadventures. But at least these mistakes will surface when the time comes to add up the corporate bottom line. In the public service this never happens: Mirabel, Pickering, urea-formaldehyde, pay-TV, everything must be swallowed without a word by employees who will tell each other: "I knew this would happen," while having to hear the public complain: "These stupid bureaucrats." "It is still the army. The good bureaucrat is an obedient bureaucrat. Saying 'Yes sir' is still the only way to survive," said a high-ranking official.

The Fragmented Bureaucrat
The third clash of reason with passion occurred over the problem of co-ordination within the public service. This had become necessary because of ever-increasing state intervention which had been planned and centralized by the control agencies. Co-ordination was achieved, it clarified countless situations and subdued countless little bureaucratic empires. In this sense it was a success. But it was achieved at the cost of countless changes that transformed work in the public service in a way that was not entirely beneficial.

Time—a Scarce Commodity

The increasing complexity of decision-making and control processes altered the workday at the top levels of the hierarchy. Senior bureaucrats had to divide their time between the activities of their own departments and the requirements of interdepartmental co-ordination. As with ministers who saw the time necessary for political activities gobbled up by Cabinet meetings, deputy ministers, their associates and their senior officials, had to cut back on the time allocated for day-to-day business in order to attend endless interdepartmental meetings. In the course of an enquiry conducted by the Treasury Board at the deputy ministers' level, one of them said: "There are no doubts in my mind that the processes in the federal government for designing and monitoring systems, strategies and structures have taken on a life of their own."[12] Another one said: "I have the feeling of having accomplished nothing else, of being useless as far as my department is concerned. I no longer know whom I serve: a self-centred and self-destructive system or a minister."

The first consequence of this daily requirement of fighting on several fronts at once was a time schedule which verged on madness, a situation which drew a sympathetic remark from someone in the private sector: "At the executive level, individuals are overloaded beyond belief."[13] The second consequence which was not so evident but more important was that the boss gradually became invisible, an abstract entity, someone who devoted little time to his subordinates or to managing his office and who in turn was hardly known by them. Interdepartmental mobility, crucial for career purposes, compounded the problem: from the employees' perspective, the top of the hierarchy became devoid of real people, of identifiable persons.

The Fragmented Product

As the image of the boss dissolved so did the image of the product. The process was hastened by the growing number of producers and by the growing number of "passions" which were allowed to intervene.

Whenever a program or decision is being discussed around a table, whether in the private or public sector, participants are also discussing territories, prerogatives and egos. This is as much a part of the dynamics of any organization, as flesh and spirit are forever joined; only Kant believed that pure reason would flow from a tribunal of great minds in search of Truth. In the course of these discussions, people trade IOUs, and they settle their accounts sometimes courteously, sometimes discreetly, sometimes even viciously.

These things, it must be repeated, are common to both public and private sectors. The solidarity of the public service, whereby bureaucrats are all united to defend their own interests, is a myth. It must be understood that there are a myriad of interests and territories, some of which may be in open conflict. Unity is found only in the collective rejection of anyone who does not play according to the rules of the game, or rather the rules of war. Nevertheless, the rivalries and the harmonization of conflicting interests in the public sector is not comparable to what happens in the private sector.

Conflicts there are of a different nature. The same is true of co-ordination. When two executives in the same firm are at odds and reconciliation proves impossible, they will fight to the end, until one of them resigns, is fired or demoted.

The winner then has a clear field to pursue his ideas, and the market place will provide ultimate judgment. In the public service, there is and there never will be any such thing as a clear field. Dismissals and demotions are practically unknown at certain levels. In this respect, writing about British bureaucracy, Hugh Heclo and Aaron Wildavsky have commented: "They know that today's passionate concern will give way to tomorrow's irrepressible cause and that the gain involved in one current issue must be balanced against the cost of souring relationships for future concerns. . . The citizens who are to be served and problems that must be met may slowly recede, viewed from the small end of the telescope, distant, blurry and easily blinked away."[14] The most serious drawback is that no cutback will ever arise spontaneously out of the bureaucratic will—cutting back is a decision.

Nor are the stakes ever really the same. The success of any product on the market brings together personally all those who have co-ordinated its production. It has forced them not to go too far in a variety of compromises, those that are intended to please, to avoid breaking too many eggs, to prevent dear old John from wasting millions duplicating what dear old Jack did because everyone likes him, or something of a similar sort. These situations exist in private enterprise, perhaps more often than the public suspects, but there is also that fragile thing called reality which shows up as a faint, almost imperceptible tap on the shoulder, causing one to stop before it's too late. If one fails to stop, economic retribution occurs in the form of bankruptcy. However, in bureaucracy the notion of a common danger is remote and abstract. The public servant might otherwise be face to face with an impossible scenario: the government threatened with bankruptcy. It is a scenario that no one cares to explore. Accordingly, anything goes: hanging on to an obsolete program, pleasing an amiable wimp, letting bureaucratic empires thrive or launching new ones. Means become ends.

The prevailing sentiment is that the system can obsorb almost anything, that personal blunders are never serious because one compares an individual to a gigantic organization and the loss of a few million with total resources that come to billions of dollars. This is exactly the view expressed by 78% of young Canadians who believe that stealing from the government by cheating or falsifying income tax returns is much less serious than stealing from an individual, or that shoplifting in a big department store is not comparable to the same offense in a small corner grocery. The larger the system, the smaller the personal responsibility. This kind of attitude is common in bureaucracy where it is easier to ignore waste, incompetence, duplication and outright dishonesty, than to say no or to come out and fight. The size of the system obscures the cause and effect relationships that are more readily apparent in small firms where the failure of one employee can cause the ruin of all.

This generalized indifference to productivity and to product quality was the hardest thing to accept for a newcomer who was recruited from private enterprise to head a team in a large department. Using his management training he immediately wanted to make his team more productive and to initiate thoroughgoing reforms such as counteracting empire-building, demoting lethargic workers, scolding the chronically tardy; in other words to assess performance as in private enterprise. "It was a revolution. Everyone was scandalized, and a delegation immediately went up to the deputy minister's office. The next week I was fired," he said. Another immigrant from private enterprise tried, but only once, to talk productivity: "My staff wrote to their member of Parliament who got in touch with my deputy minister." Since then she has been languishing in Ottawa with a reputation for being a poor administrator.

The danger with bureaucracy is that co-ordination and compromise are never related to the possibility of bankruptcy. As a result staff meetings in government lose sight of the end product. Alliances are forged according to the number of people involved. Meetings are taken up with the beliefs of participants, their mandates, their empires large and small, and by the attempt to come to some kind of agreement that will give satisfaction to all. A typical Ottawa joke is that a camel is really a horse put together by a committee. This explains why the Auditor General has found so many camels trotting about on the snow drifts. In his report for 1983, he wrote:

> A department had printed maps for nearly 100 years, but was questioned by a central service department whose mandate included the provision of printing services. The dispute went on for seven years and according to one study, resulted in unnecessary costs of over $900,000. This case illustrates how difficult it is to improve productivity when departmental mandates clash and when the means of obtaining one's goal are contested.[15]

A former director general of the Treasury Board commented in a similar vein, "There are just not a few cases. . . and you have to play the game; if you don't, you lose the tiny bit of power that you must have to be effective in your program. . . ."

To this specific problem we must add the no less specific one of a group of bureaucratic managers whose sole product is the enforcement of bureaucratic regulations (we will see which ones later). It is easy to see then why administrative co-ordination always runs the risk of being like a complicated set of mirrors. This was brilliantly brought out in a study by J. Pressman and A. Wildavsky on a series of public works projects in Oakland.[16] They found that it was necessary to go through some 70 bureaucratic green lights, thereby raising the odds of obtaining all administrative go-aheads at the same time to one in a million.

This means that in any bureaucracy, the possibilities of straying from initial goals are proportionate to the number of participants authorized to intervene, with the process inevitably giving rise to unimaginable procrastination and pettiness.

From the 1970s onwards, the opportunities of things going wrong rose with the number of sorcerer's apprentices, assistant chefs, apprentice pastry cooks, and various helpers invading the kitchen. We already saw that the rush towards the upper levels, confirmed in the data for 1984, increased the number of people allowed to have their say at one point or another in bureaucratic decisions. As shown in Table 18, which applies to decision-makers in the national capital region, 55 per cent of the men are at the middle management level. It is true that many analysts without any managerial functions are included in this category, but as one official explained, "Even the analysts try to persuade you that their ideas should be considered. It is an ongoing battle of dealing with egos, and egos, and egos, from the bottom to the top, and when you go home you cannot even talk to your spouse and deal with the problems of your children. You have had enough already; you cannot take more smothering, coaxing, persuading. . . you are psychologically drained."

Proliferating cooks spoiled the broth most often in the relations between departments and central agencies, where age, attitudes and inexperience were countless points of friction.

The co-ordinating process established by the Privy Council Office and by the Prime Minister's Office never displayed the expected flexibility and detachment. The former never became the kind of super secretariat that had been imagined. Nor did the latter ever become the central switchboard that had been initially anticipated. Certain people could never restrain themselves and they fussed to the extent that departmental decisions became opportunities for interaction, reaction or prevention.

Young officials often displayed excessive zeal. They had little to lose because they had not yet been integrated into the bureaucratic system of IOUs and backscratching, and they had everything to gain by attracting the notice of the Prime Minister himself. Some of them used and abused this kind of strategy, provoking general gnashing of teeth and evoking in the memory of many war veterans a long forgotten and unpublishable vocabulary. A Treasury Board official relates one of these encounters with the Privy Council Office, "Once I had an extremely frustrating experience with PCO. I was working on a project involving senior officials in various departments. I had worked out the details with the deputy ministers of all the departments and with the ministry responsible. So I sent the proposal off to PCO for their stamp of approval. I was rejected by some pipsqueak fresh out of graduate school because there were "jurisdictional problems". . . . Those guys draw the wagon in a circle to protect their own. But this thing really infuriated me. . . "[17]

Not that the Treasury Board was always an innocent victim. This time the complaint comes from the deputy minister of an operational department:

> It's a queer world where those who have some competence and experience (in departments) must train and educate those who do not (in central agencies); who thereby gain the competence and experience to lay down procedures and control those who taught them! It's an even queerer world where some relatively junior inexperienced official in the Treasury Board Secretariat can exercise an effect on my department which would not be possible by a more senior competent officer inside the department, and to overcome the effect of that junior inexperienced TBS Officer requires the concerted attention of several senior members of departmental management including the Deputy Head.[18]

The situation was also extremely frustrating for officials in the central agencies who were trying to co-ordinate ideas and territorial claims for presentation to the Cabinet. In 1981 one of them, a former employee of the Ministry of State for Social Development, wrote a play entitled Don't Despair, Fonctionnaire. It was about a bilingual unit struggling through the preparation of a memorandum for the Cabinet. Peter, the main character, tells it like it is: "We've got three days for the real work. The rest of the time we are getting input from every nitpick-minded bureaucrat in the department who wants a say."

This explains many delays which the consumers of the bureaucratic product are unable to explain rationally other than pointing to the laziness of public servants who let files gather dust while they endlessly sip coffee in the departmental cafeteria. In most cases, it is the exact opposite: what slows things down is overwork.

The need for co-ordination obviously changed the rules of the bureaucratic game. A new ethic came to rule, to the great consternation of the older bureaucrats, who retired with relief and left Ottawa for sunnier climes.

Situational Ethics

During the postwar years, simple rules governed the life of the average public servant: to please the minister or his immediate boss for many long years, given the rather low rate of turnover.

During the 1960s, the object was still to please. But the game was rather ephemeral (the duration of a program), and faster (speed up the real estate game of location, location, location). The point was to be at the right place at the right time for the launching of a new bureaucratic empire. For this generation, playing the odds was the key to success.

In the 1970s the game hardened as it became more sophisticated.

o   It hardened as the growing number of entries at the same level made competition all the stiffer. Table 18 describes that phenomenon.

o   What complicated matters was that a successful career no longer rested on the ambitious public servant's ability to please his minister or his immediate superior, but on the way he made himself visible to the central agencies. This was the case for those who had access to Cabinet documents and to the control agencies of that period. It was also true for management in finance and personnel.

The art of navigation took over from competence. The bureaucratic ethic became a systemic one: more abstract and insensitive than that of a smaller group. The cleverest ones sometimes reached the realm of pure abstracton. They practised the art of moving from department to department, from agency to agency, of pursuing their careers without ever producing a product. They reproduced the

107

Table 18: Federal Employees, National Capital Region, 1984, by Hierarchical Levels and by Sex

	Men	Women	Totals
Upper Management	7,133	985	8,118
Middle Management	12,901	3,754	16,655
Officers	8,235	7,191	15,426
Support	8,123	17,252	25,375
Total	36,392	29,182	65,574

Source: Public Service Commission, unpublished data.

lesson of Voltaire's young marquis who could neither read, write, compose nor hunt, but who succeeded because, according to the author: "All he needed was to know how to dance."

Indeed, the gates opened wide for those who managed the system and knew how to negotiate on such a large scale, but not so wide for the managers of individual programs who knew how to make them work. This can be verified by comparing the upper echelons of the central agencies, where the system's navigators are found, with personnel of operational departments, such as Public Works, for example.

Table 19: Treasury Board and Public Works Employees, National Capital Region, by Hierarchical Levels, 1984

	Treasury Board	Public Works
Upper Management	400	297
Middle Management	105	509
Officers	75	578
Support	176	1,284
Totals	756	2,668

Source: Public Service Commission, unpublished data.

One can observe that more than half (52.7 per cent) of Treasury Board staff are at the top of the pyramid, while the percentage drops to 11 in the case of Public Works. Without passing judgment on the shape of these pyramids, it is obvious that chances for advancement are much greater in an organization where people in upper management are very numerous. For any ambitious person in Ottawa, this is a very important consideration.

The hierarchy stimulated interdepartmental mobility of the SX group (now EX), many of whom were quite rightly persuaded that career advancement would be more rapid after a time spent in the central agencies. This did little to improve a bureaucratic product that had already been severely devalued.

A Profound Malaise

It would be a mistake to interpret the foregoing comments as a commonplace demonstration of bureaucratic greed whose sole purpose is to complicate the decision making process in order to build paper empires at the expense of the government and of Canadians. Undeniably, many have shamelessly profited from bureaucratic inflation. But there is more to it than that.

Part of the growing complexity of decision making is due to the fact that the bureaucracy as a whole reflects the multiplicity, ambiguity, and even contradictory nature of Canadian values, as well as the possibilities of conflict among diverse groups whose very diversity has become more pronounced. The bureaucracy in charge of programs for the public was gradually given the task of conciliator: it must constantly try to reconcile all those who want hard-line industrial-type productivity, those who insist on specific and costly requirements such as having documents issued in two languages, and those who defend special interest groups. Sometimes, it is the very same groups who want everything at once, leaving the bureaucracy with the difficult task of bridging idealism and practicality, of translating expectations into reality: good roads but no more taxes, acknowledgement of individual rights without any relaxation of the social order.

The slowness, the complexity and the contradictions of

bureaucratic decision making are sometimes the reflection of a national culture, a culture whose thoughts are turning increasingly upon itself, and which asks the federal government for explanations and guidance. Whether we like it or not, we find ourselves with an army of technocrats mediating between popular expectations and their fulfilment. This suggests the hypothesis that part of the aggressiveness shown by Canadians towards the federal bureaucracy is due to this situation of being between two chairs, a situation which no one really wants to look at. If the dream can't be made to come true, then the culprit must be the bureaucratic donkey.

There was also, without any doubt, political complicity in the treasure hunt of the 1970s. It was an active complicity in the sense that a large number of careers were launched directly by politicians, particularly a whole group of former ministers' assistants who were parachuted to high levels of the bureaucracy, thereby provoking the same kind of resentment experienced by people who have been patiently waiting in line at the movies for some time and who see some people cutting into line and moving directly to the ticket booth. There was also passive complicity in that politicians were never really interested in the internal problems of the public service.

The orientation of our culture in general is towards expansion and bureaucrats are as much a part of it as the average Canadian. Because government bureaucracy is not tested by the same kind of fire as private enterprise, its quality is mostly dependent on the superego of bureaucrats which is itself ultimately derived from the values and the education found in our culture. So it was with the frugal and self-effacing mandarins of an earlier age; they were not exceptional heroes selected for service to the country but simply the representatives of attitudes and ideas which were prevalent at that time.

It was the same in 1960 and 1970. The young turks of that period represented an entire culture. They were educated in universities where discipline and academic evaluation had changed radically. They were cast from a mental mould which changed the face of the country. They had expectations and ethics common to everybody. Placed within a structure which was expanding rapidly, without guard rails, they

110

showed the same reflexes and the same ambitions as any employee of the private sector, with the difference that combative energies were often deflected towards territorial expansion—empire-building—instead of being focused on the product itself. The idea is not to whitewash the bureaucracy but to bring out the fact that such an important sub-group does not emerge out of the void and that its attitudes say a great deal about all of us. Bureaucracies are the mirrors of the societies they happen to be in, and no one really likes what he sees there.

In 1980, the situation had become rather uncomfortable for the bureaucratic world of Ottawa. Similarly, social and economic trends were alarming Canadians who were coming out of the euphoria of their younger days and wondering if they could continue taking for granted the standard of living they had always enjoyed.

The situation was becoming particularly uncomfortable in Ottawa where the limits to complexity in decision making and to continued expansion were becoming increasingly clear. Middle management levels were overcrowded and pushing rivalries beyond the tolerable level. The rapid promotion of young managers had blocked access to the summit of the pyramid for many years to come. Career options were curtailed, thereby putting even more pressure on competitivenes.

There was also considerable discomfort from an ethical point of view. Direct or indirect participation by a large number of federal employees in political decisions was a source of cynicism. Too many employees were in the ambiguous situation of knowing more than the average Canadian but less than the politicians. It had become impossible for them to hang on to an old, simple and innocent faith, but at the same time they did not have all the knowledge allowing them to put decisions in a proper perspective. In other words, they held only fragments of power in the political process, where proximity to the summit simultaneously triggered cynicism, a desire to change things, a willingness to participate, as well as an inferiority complex. Given the very large number of government employees, there would be a great deal to say about the circumstances that created this situation: of a long-neglected, socio-political group which would have to redefine itself in the years to come in relation to itself, to politics and to Canadians.

The situation was also uncomfortable for government employees from day-to-day. There was an excessive workload which many considered to be totally useless, or "a heavy ritual devoid of meaning," as one deputy minister put it. The upper levels of the hierarchy were spread too thin and were intellectually exhausted by the very length of their working day. "The meetings are the worst. I spend three quarters of my day at meetings, negotiating endlessly. Maybe it's the price for democracy. . . but what a price!" said one senior official.

And as if this were not enough to bring about what one Ottawa doctor described as "the highest stress levels in the country", conditions across Canada were changing and there were mounting pressures everywhere calling on the government to tame the monster it had created. "Welcome to the 1980s", said Pierre Trudeau the night of the Liberal restoration after the brief Conservative interlude. It was merely a figure of speech. The beginning of the 1980s threw Canadians into a fright: the future was no longer what it seemed to be. The party was over.

5: THE PARTY'S OVER!

Ottawa-Hull 1980

At the beginning of this decade, the national capital was still prosperous, appearing all the more comfortable in its prosperity as the rest of the country was in the throes of the worst recession since the 1930s. Obviously the two slumps were not comparable in scope or in terms of human suffering. But the private sector had just absorbed a painful psychological blow forcing it to rearrange its priorities and re-shape management organization. Higher yields were squeezed out of lagging investments, the superfluous was eliminated, staff was laid off, and everything was cut to the bone in the sure knowledge that in order to survive one had to be lean.

It was about that time, in 1981, that the Public Service Commission announced that the number of federal employees would increase by a further 3 per cent during the year. Public reaction was so hostile that the government was forced to take action. In 1982, it launched the so-called 6 and 5 program, putting a ceiling on salary increases for the public service for the next two years. Given the double-digit rate of inflation at the time, this amounted to a salary cut. Public servants were strangely silent; they knew very well that Canadians were not in any mood for murmuring from the ranks. There was among them an awareness, reinforced by feelings of guilt, that job security was the most precious thing they had in this period of high unemployment, something which compensated for any salary loss (which, as it happened, was quite small compared to the one which was visited on provincial employees in Quebec).

The mood was certainly not one of panic and had little resemblance to what was happening in the private sector. As can be expected of any bureaucracy, the federal public service was five years behind the times: it was just ending its adaptation to the period of rapid growth which had overtaken it earlier. It was not at all prepared for a period of "negative growth", as they say. There were a lot of buzzwords like "downsizing" and "trimming", but it was all talk and no action. It was a perfect illustration of the thesis put forward by Robert K. Merton and Michel Crozier that bureaucracies "adapt to a disadapted situation."

According to Michel Crozier, this disadaptment is written into any organization which cannot react quickly because of its size, which guards the forces of inertia in any society (possibly playing a positive role in this respect), and which is never motivated in the same way as other organizations whose survival depends on rapid adaptation to changing circumstances such as take place in the open market.

Another characteristic could be added, based on Parkinson's Law: the propensity of the internal administrative apparatus to eat up the energy which should be directed towards the outside, and its extraordinary ability to rise from the ashes.

These characteristics apply to the Canadian public service as it was in the past. After 1980 they are to be found as an inverted image.

In 1960, the aging bureaucracy had to respond to more insistent demands for programs, personnel and funds. Its head was still in the 1950s and it was quietly digesting the postwar influx of new employees. Bound by its own regulations, it could not move by itself. What was needed to change the regulations and adapt to a new reality was the political intervention taking place in the wake of the Glassco Report.

It was done with some delay, but the enthusiasm with which things were done for a while more than compensated for it. In 1980, just as the public service was digesting its second great influx of employees and suffering from heartburn, society was asking it to reverse the process of growth and cut back on its numbers. But it could not do this by itself, since it was tied up again in new regulations which, this time, were adapted solely to growth and spending.

It is ironic that in 1960 the public service should starve from not being able to hire additional employees, while in 1980 it was undergoing a slow death for not being able to slough off employees and economize.

What happened?

Who Controls What?

The great administrative reforms launched between 1965 and 1975, which seemed to be a liberation from the old shackles, were launched on the basis of the Glassco Report. But were they optical illusions due to changes in vocabulary (sometimes sufficient to make people believe that reality has changed)? Did they produce only a temporary liberation? We don't know. But in any event, far from providing managers with greater initiative, the internal administration of the public service weighted itself down from year to year with the result that, by 1980, federal bureaucrats were in the same situation as their predecessors: they were paralysed by regulations many of which no longer made any sense.

In terms of personnel management the bureaucratic machinery was just as creaky as it ever was in spite of the reforms introduced as a result of the Glassco Report. True, responsibility for staffing was handed over to the departments; this does not mean that the merit principle was abandoned even though, as we shall see later, its application was often only a matter of form. In addition, the volume of staffing had continued to grow during the 1970s, representing, on average, an annual rate of turnover, reclassification, reorganization or transfer for a quarter of the employees of each department. Imperceptibly, delays in staffing came to be as long as those of the 1950s. According to the official reports of the Public Service Commission, ninety days were required to staff a position; but according to the unofficial impressions of senior staff, six-month delays were closer to the truth. Moreover, it was impossible to assess the performance of individual employees or to fire them.

Financial management bogged down with cost-benefit and cost-efficiency analysis and with what was called the "alphabet soup" of financial control practices, such as PPB, OPMS and MBO. These were established during the planning frenzy of the Trudeau years, and they quickly became ritual procedures whereby departments renewed money requirements from one year to the next, filled in the stipulated schedules, all the while tailoring their requests on paper to whichever way political winds seemed to be blowing, not revealing their real intentions, and trying to fend off whatever blows might be coming their way.[1]

The bureaucratic machinery could not cope with the problem of staff representativeness. French-speaking people and other minorities quickly grasped that the programs set in motion to enhance their status had only a symbolic value. The only beneficiary was the fantastic administration responsible for their implementation.

Controls proliferated during the second half of the 1970s when it became clear to everyone that something had to be done. Accountability, review and assessment were the buzzwords of the decade. The number of steps and procedures required for program evaluation reached more than twenty, and reviews came so thick and fast that program managers saw their effective working hours eroded even further.

A confidential study estimated that one third of government employees in Ottawa had purely administrative functions, as opposed to operational ones consisting of the implementation of programs and contacts with the public. Such an estimate is a conservative one and does not take into account administrative overhead, such as the cost of maintenance employees, some of whom work under contract and who must sometimes be housed, fed and even clothed.

Unverifiable estimates show that since the war, the purely administrative staff in the public service multiplied by ten while the entire service has grown only by four, an illustration of Parkinson's Law, if ever there was one. Twenty years after the Glassco Report, the situation is worse than ever. For every ten line managers who are in contact with the public, who are implementing specific programs, or who are out in the field (engineers and meteorologists), there are three staff managers whose task it is to ride herd on the others.

There is something fascinating in these bureaucratic outgrowths which are characteristic of all large organizations and which confirm some of the theories advanced in the bestselling book Small Is Beautiful. They can, however, be seen from a different angle, as tertiary outgrowths which, despite being parasitic in certain respects, also create a large number of jobs. It is as if the public service reproduced the tendencies of the labour force where certain areas of the tertiary sector were ballooning.

Another volume would be required to examine how the public service grew heavy and cumbersome. But for present purposes, the key aspects of these bureaucratic outgrowths are staffing and financing, the bottlenecks of the 1980s which are preventing adaptation to a new reality.

Till Death Do Us Part!

Following the Glassco Report, part of the staffing responsibility was delegated to individual departments in the hope of reducing the delays associated with the centralization of this function in the hands of the Public Service Commission. It removed one step in the long process of application of the merit principle for every candidate. The move was well received at the time, except for some former members of the Commission who predicted a general inflation of classifications, something which did in fact happen.

But this delegation of authority had little to do with the freedom of private sector managers to hire those who seemed best for the job. In 1985, as in 1955, the merit principle is still the sacred cow of the public service. Canadians have not changed their views one iota on this matter, if one can believe the negative reactions that greeted the political appointments which constituted Pierre Trudeau's parting gift to the nation. The requirements of 1935, 1945 and 1955 were still in force: the proof of just treatment of employees on the basis of merit

117

rather than of their political leanings and the guarantee that no one can be fired for belonging to a political party.

This means that, in spite of a delegation of authority, the hiring, classification and evaluation of personnel must go through a number of strict and complicated steps against which a private sector manager would rebel. But they make sense even if they are followed only as a matter of form. What happens behind the scenes is not so important; however, the symbolism of the purity of the merit principle which we display is. It plays the same role in Canadian bureaucracy as the nuptial sheets in Mediterranean countries which are displayed as a proof of virginity; whether the blood be human or that of a chicken whose neck was wrung at the last moment, it is the idea of the blood that matters.

It was a short-lived liberation. Staffing operations during the years of growth were so numerous that the effort spent on this activity in each department soon ate up the time and the energy which had been freed by decentralization.

As Table 20 shows, the public service proceeded with more than a million staffing operations between 1970 and 1979, of which more than a quarter (298,281) had to do with employees entering the service. In addition, during those ten years it processed almost 700,000 internal staffing operations in the form of reclassifications, transfers, promotions (half of all cases), demotions and changes of category.

Knowing that outside recruitment and inside promotions require, in principle, a notice of competition, an examination of an average of twenty applications, a process of selection by a panel of at least three members, and posting the results with notice of appeal, one can estimate that there have been one million applications during this decade, all of which have to be calculated in terms of hours of work and of paperwork. Considering only appointments from outside the service, this would mean that six million Canadians have filed job applications with the public service at one time or another during this decade, which comes to possibly half the labour force, if one does not take multiple applications into account.

Table 20: Number of External and Internal Appointments by the Public Service, 1970 to 1979

	External Appointments	Internal Appointments	Total
1970	23,055	30,279	53,334
1971	27,706	38,969	66,675
1972	38,568	49,916	88,484
1973	38,979	59,536	98,515
1974	46,567	78,232	124,799
1975	36,251	90,920	127,171
1976	30,201	91,031	121,232
1977	22,427	112,559	134,986
1978	19,224	103,031	122,255
1979	15,293	98,756	114,049
Total	298,271	753,229	1,051,500

Source: Public Service Commission, Annual Reports, 1970 to 1979.

This leads us to believe that whenever Canadians voice their contempt for the public service, what they are really expressing is sour grapes. One can smell the sulphurous fumes of envy.

Nobody has ever estimated the cost of the voluminous correspondence related to staffing. It would be worthwhile analysing it as meticulously as an accountant. The very number of applications indicates the great volume of work which falls on the shoulders of government departments, and the burden in time, energy and number of employees which this enormous organization must carry in order to administer itself.

The question is how did the public service manage to proceed with so many hirings and promotions during the 1960s and 1970s, in spite of the strict and complicated regulations surrounding merit and the very volume of staffing required.

The explanation is a simple one: the application of the law had changed. We should not forget that laws and principles have no existence by themselves outside the people who put them into effect, with a spirit that may change from one period to the next. True, there was no longer the inhibiting authority of the Treasury Board on classifications, and that of the Public Service Commission on all attempts to promote or reclassify. In this sense, the Glassco Report had been a liberating influence. But all it did was eliminate one bureaucratic step signifying a gain in time of possibly three months. Other changes were more significant. There was a general transformation of mentalities whose enthusiasm distorted the rules of the merit principle in order to share in the current euphoric mood expressed by the slogan "grow and prosper." The procedures governing evaluations, classifications and examinations, all of which tend to throttle merit, gave rise to diversified and advantageous interpretations of the law.

Vanity Fair

One of the most advantageous interpretations of the merit principle had to do with job specifications which govern the classification and reclassification of federal employees. For federal employees it is the basis on which their salaries are determined and is therefore of considerable importance.

Following the reform of the classification system, an attempt was made to define tasks as objectively as possible by relating salaries to those paid in the private sector. The sole responsibility of the government's Pay Research Bureau is to keep up-to-date comparative tables of wages paid in the two sectors. The only exception to parity is the upper levels of the hierarchy whose salaries are often below those for corresponding jobs in private enterprise. The reason for this is purely psychological: no politician and no taxpayer would ever accept the idea that a "servant", no matter how overburdened with work and responsibility, could earn that kind of money.

As we saw, the old public service had created its own little world apart from the private sector, and was emprisoned in a complicated system of job specifications which were constantly revised in the light of changing needs. The system was grossly inefficient and unjust, but its very unwieldiness gave it enormous stability. Once a job position had been classified, the Comptroller of the Treasury and the Public Service Commission made sure that the classification order was engraved in stone and that any modification would become practically impossible. "The Commission drove a hard bargain every time a department asked for a revision. In exchange it demanded that two other posts either be downgraded or eliminated altogether. The department gained a high level job but the bureaucratic pyramid became more slender," explained a former public servant.

Everything changed with the second wave of expansion. The job specification system was modeled on the private sector. Classifications were combined and simplified. But this improvement had its price: job contents became more volatile. The private sector, shaken earlier by growth and by technology, had already experienced this kind of problem. Experimentation had produced countless new specialities. Moreover, it was difficult to describe and classify certain jobs that had no identifiable product and were restricted to the public service, such as social research and political analysis, jobs which happened to be overrepresented during the 1970s.

The inevitable happened. In the absence of rigid criteria, recognized productivity standards, and a central authority which might be able to apply the brakes to the whole process, and on the faith of a generation which believed it knew everything, job descriptions became subjective, inflated and interminably wordy.

There have been numerous accounts of the impact of this verbal inflation. A recent Treasury Board report noted that 34 per cent of all positions were overclassified. Hubert Laframboise and Doug Hartle have been the most open commentators on what the former has described as a "torrent of words" unconnected with reality, whether at the time of hiring (when the job is classified) or as the reclassification of a permanent employee is under study (the job itself is reclassified by means of a promotion). A lot of people still remember the job description which a lowly departmental adviser wrote for himself and which seemed more applicable to a cabinet minister. And these same people were horrified when the particular job description was approved by the responsible authority, boosting the ambitious adviser to the level of director.

How could this happen? A person in authority has every advantage in swelling the ranks of his immediate subordinates, because he himself will then be able to ask for a reclassification of his own position on the grounds that he has a larger number of ranking officials to supervise. The public service displayed the same inflationary proclivities in grades, evaluations and perceptions as did the educational system of the day. In the course of a meeting of the Advisory Group on Executive Level Compensation in the Public Service, Allen Lambert, former chairman of the Toronto-Dominion Bank, expressed thinly veiled dismay at the way top executives were evaluated: "An astounding 63 per cent were said to be discharging their responsibilities in a superior or outstanding fashion. Personnel experts generally consider that, in any sizable group of individuals, it is statistically impossible that almost two thirds should be performing their jobs in an exceptional or above-average manner."[2] It was psychologically more difficult for a manager to say no than for an impersonal body like the Treasury Board or the Public Service Commission. Because of the great mobility within the system, the indulgent manager did not have to suffer the consequences of his laxness. There was a general impression during the 1960s and 1970s that the system could easily absorb all minor lapses of that kind.

The results can be seen from the number of promotions granted: 300,000 between 1970 and 1979, some of which resulted from reclassification.

This massive upgrading had serious consequences, not so much for the public purse which supported far more scandalous expenditures, but for the morale of the public servants who had to live with the situation. Job inflation made them skeptical, and they learned to make the distinction between official statements and reality which they saw as being very different. Thus, the Auditor General's annual report for 1982 notes that 60 per cent of all public servants were very skeptical about the relationship between the official description of their tasks and what they were actually doing.

The massive upgrading of that period also made them cynical because, as one observer remarked, it favoured those who could be pushy, or, according to another, those who "spent more time polishing their CVs, their job descriptions and their contacts than in actually working, while the losers were the hardworking ones, those who did not know how to manipulate words, or who simply did not have the time to spare." The situation made public servants suspicious of one another, each observing the other and trying not to be overtaken. It stimulated rivalry at the middle management level and increased the general sense of discomfort. But no one became wiser for all that because no one could afford to lag behind.

Bogus Examinations

Another loose and self-serving adaptation of the merit principle took place in connection with the examinations that supposedly ensure the hiring or the promotion of the most qualified candidate. The model used is the academic one, and it requires no special practice. The decision is made solely on the basis of examination results, although in principle there should be a year's probation after which the jury's decision is either confirmed or put aside. But the probation is not a rigourous one; only a minuscule proportion get the famous pink slip that puts an end to their public service career.

The whole procedure is a long and complicated one. It begins with the publication in the two official languages of a notice of examination which may be open to outsiders, to public servants only or even to employees of a single department. Most of the time, the examination consists of an interview conducted by a jury. The decision is posted for fifteen days, giving unsuccessful candidates enough time to lodge an appeal should they believe the decision is unjust, discriminatory, or affected by some procedural irregularity.

In practical terms, this means that a manager in the public service cannot, like his opposite number in the private sector, offer a job directly to the person he feels is the best qualified for it. In principle this means that he cannot dispose of public offices which have been entrusted to him and offer them to his friends and protégés. He cannot fire incompetents without going by the decision of a panel similar to the one which hired them or promoted them in the first place.

However, as any procedure which happens to be too broad and

abstract, this one is open to all kinds of manipulations for hiring earmarked candidates. It is possible to hire someone for a period of six months without any examination, to cause this specific job to be transformed into a permanent position, and then to post notice for an examination in which the candidate who has already been on the job for six months has the best chance of being successful in properly answering the questions the jury will be putting to him. In the case of a promotion, it is possible to avoid examinations by having the position reclassified. It is also possible to pave the way for an earmarked candidate by making a preselection which will place him ahead of others who have no chance of success. It is also possible to affect the decision of the jury by using influence and cashing IOUs, by playing on the nerves of undesiderable candidates, and by taking advantage of the ambiguity surrounding the choice of a candidate solely on the basis of an interview.

Some public service managers are past masters in the art of doing exactly as they please, while others are not as skilful or are indifferent to this question of hiring. No one really knows how many there are in each group. But the answers given by some fifty government employees chosen at random show that three-quarters believe most examinations are biased right from the start; some even thought this was acceptable. Half of them believe that public service managers are acting in good faith, "only trying to prevent the organization from imposing somebody on them who is not good, only trying to be efficient."

Given the large number of staffing operations, the 1970s were no doubt a period of experimentation regarding examinations, a period during which federal employees learned to adapt to the new situation. "Just by looking at the job description, I can tell you if there is already a candidate in the job or if someone has already been chosen. . . .It's all in the wording. In most cases I don't even bother applying," boasted one employee.

The adaptation of a rigid principle, solidified by years of use, to changing circumstances touched only one aspect of the merit principle, the positive one which is control of hiring and promoting. Its negative aspect, firing and demoting, was completely ignored. The reason is a simple one: only the positive aspect was of any significance to an expanding bureaucracy. It was not that these situations never occurred: in fact there were 500 dismissals and 2,200 demotions during 1984. But they represent only 0.7 per cent and 3 per cent of the appointments made during that year. One might also say, but no one will actually dare, that these figures represent the real rate of incompetence, or the Peter Principle, in the public service. Another reason, which is just as simple and perhaps more trivial, is that the candidate's full co-operation and complicity are guaranteed when hiring or promoting; no one has ever lodged a complaint for an undeserved promotion or for being hired on the basis of a biased examination. Whenever the opposite takes place, it generates noisy hostility: no one is really expected to applaud his own dismissal or demotion in the name of justice.

Obviously, the rigidity of the merit principle lends itself to manipulation in a positive or negative sense, but "it is infinitely more difficult" in the latter case. Once appointed, a public servant is deemed to be competent until there has been proof to the contrary, something which is usually very difficult to provide. Proof of incompetence would require a clear definition of the work to be performed, which in most cases is impossible. It would also be necessary to have a look into the employee's career file, and there is every likelihood that at some point an easy-going evaluator gave him reason to believe that he was indeed very competent. On the other hand, the employee can always claim that his incompetence can in fact be attributed to a superior who failed to explain his responsibilities in a sufficiently clear manner.

"If you want to get rid of someone, you have to work at it for one year and put two of your best officers on the case full-time. . . . It is not worth it," said one official. Consequently manipulation will become sneaky, as in guerrilla warfare. It will not result in eliminating the dead wood but in trying to pass it on to some other service, some other department, some professional training program, always within the public service.

In the most desperate situations, explained a former official, "I

125

figured it was less costly in terms of the time wasted to completely reorganize my one-hundred-strong service in order to eliminate with every appearance of rationality both the position held by an incompetent and the incompetent himself than trying to get rid of him directly. In my time I proceeded with three massive reorganizations for three people who should never have reached the level they had in the first place, but who were there nonetheless." Another one explained, "I just recommended my guy for a promotion in another department. It's dirty, but it's the only way." Of course, this employee's position will become all the more unchallengeable because of this recommendation, and the vicious circle becomes even more vicious.

This kind of internal problem would not be too serious if the organization had continued to expand and had been able to relegate the dead wood and the mistakes of the past to one of those multiple sidetracks that every wave of expansion seems to generate. It should be added that the problem somehow does not seem as acute to those who must put up with it on a daily basis and who entertain the hope of eventually being able to escape from this forced cohabitation with incompetence.

But whenever growth stalls, as it did at the beginning of the 1980s, the situation becomes much more serious. The public service woke up realizing that the party was over and that it could no longer run ahead of its own problems. Mobility melted like a snowball in hell: it was cut in half between 1976 and 1983, promotions dropping from 40,338 to 19,949. Employees had to be satisfied with what they had and accept the reality of rank whatever the competence and whatever youthful errors had been committed. Because of the earlier drop in the average age in the public service, there were few hopes of advancement through attrition and retirement; one half of the decision-makers in the upper levels of government were under forty years of age. There would be twenty-five long years ahead for ruminating on the past, for better or for worse.

The situation had come full circle to the point in the 1960s when the public service had been the object of the most virulent criticism as a result of its inability to adapt to changing circumstances. Public servants experienced the frustration of seeing their hands tied, and the wiser among them feared that any change in the status quo would provoke more serious errors still. "It's true that Canadians want us to cut. It is true that we would love to do something, and something good. . .but somehow, here we are. . . because it is virtually impossible to say what you think, we cannot get rid of those who deserve it in the first place. When we actually cut, it falls on some innocent group of employees who were good employees, the unlucky ones, the ones without a network of friends, the ones whose only mistake was to be at the wrong place at the wrong moment. Some days, I feel like crying. Every day I feel like quitting."

Impossible Savings

In the same manner and at the same time, the finances of the public service, which had been liberated by the Glassco Report and planned during the Trudeau era, bogged down in procedural concerns, in formalism, and in a total inability to come to terms with the new requirements of the Canadian economy. It had become impossible to economize; spending had been woven into the everyday practices of the system and was subject to the irresistible force of human motivation.

Indeed, playing the game of economy in such a system requires the personal sacrifice of each participant. This is asking a great deal from a person who realizes he might be the only one coming forward to assume that risk, deciding on a course of action yielding neither glory nor applause, making a gesture similar to that of the taxpayer concerned over the deficit, who decides to forward all his personal savings anonymously to the minister of finance.

It is obvious that a manager has every advantage in inflating his staff as much as possible. It is not only a question of self-promotion. It is also a question of prudence, in case he is required to make cuts. It is a necessary reflex for survival. Some fat is needed to go through periods of famine.

According to Jim Steinhart, Environment Canada had pioneered waste-cutting innovations in the government: "Yet, when major cuts started about three years ago, the programs which had already proved their value were hit just as badly as those in any other department. Such lessons get around. Even the optimists who look on the cuts as a positive event forcing inefficient sections to trim fat forget that, the second time around, there is only muscle and bone left to trim."[3]

Every manager in the public service is interested in renewing his budget estimates, even if he has not used up all the funds requested for the preceding year—"just in case." Hubert Laframboise has explained the practice under the term of "lapsophobia", the roots of which are embedded in the length of the budget cycle and in the convention that money voted by Parliament for one year cannot be carried forward to the following year if unspent. This means that a director who realizes in January that he runs the risk of not spending the amounts allocated to him will devote part of the next quarter to finding ways of quickly spending all by the end of the fiscal year. "Starting from January, contracts are falling all over the place, no matter what the subject is or the quality of the work. These things are not important. What matters is for a service director to have his budget renewed for next year," explained a consultant.

The person-year system has been set up in such a way that no distinction is made between levels or categories. A person-year is a person-year, whether it applies to a high-ranking official or an ordinary secretary. Whenever person-year cuts are decreed, managers will first cut at the lowest levels, knowing that they will be able to hire any number of temporary secretaries.

Accordingly, the public service manager, even with the best intentions, cannot make the same choices as a private sector manager who makes the maximum cuts compatible with the same quality of service. The Auditor General's 1983 report dwells on this problem at considerable length.

Everything leads back to the quagmire of merit: overpromoted or not, overclassified or not, parsimonious or spendthrift, all distinctions become blurred. The system no longer possesses any effective sticks and carrots. It is the perfect anomic situation described by a 41-year-old director general under the approving glances of his colleagues:

"You know. . . I never thought I would say it one day. . .but today I just work for my salary."

Thus, at the end of 1984, the public service had come full circle and could no longer budge on its own.

CONCLUSIONS: 1985

When the Conservatives came to power in September 1984, they inherited 225,000 person-years, about which very little was known, not even whether they had a soul. The huge organization which they now controlled exhibited the following traits and characteristics:

1. It comprised an aging population which had closed its doors to the tail end of the baby boom, to those who had been born around 1961. The 20-24 age group, which had constituted almost 13 per cent of all federal employees in 1972, was down to 7.2 per cent by 1984. The drop was even more striking in the national capital. In 1976, there had been 2,549 young men and 6,008 young women aged 20 to 24; they numbered only 760 and 2,474 in 1984.

2. The concentration of federal employees in the national capital had reached almost one third—32.2 per cent—in 1984.

3. Over a period of twenty years, this organization had experienced three successive waves of positive action (war veterans, young people and francophones) but never got around to integrating women.

4. The hierarchical structure had become distorted with heavy expansion at the middle levels, to the point where competition had increased tenfold over ten years. A period of intense mobility had just come to an end, which had left everyone dizzy and nostalgic.

5. The remuneration system inhibited responsiblity.

6. The public service was largely made of up of an anomic population which no longer paid attention to official policy statements, among whom mediocrity and excellence were constantly rubbing shoulders, which could not even distinguish between the two for lack of an identifiable product, but which insisted nevertheless on invoking the criteria and the standards of the private sector.

7. The public service was neither loved nor respected by the general population, and it had no channels to make itself heard and understood.

8. It knew very little about itself, and its thinking was founded primarily on perceptions and sometimes on misconceptions.

9. Its philosophy until now had been an unholy mixture of private sector rules, an academic ethic, and a dash of military discipline.

In the abstract world of writing and armchair intellectualism, the nine points sketched above call for immediate solutions whose simplicity is readily apparent—on paper. In reality, each solution can ricochet, giving rise to even more aggravating situations.

1. Opening its doors to the younger generation of Canadians would swell the ranks of the public service at an excessive cost. It is possible to accelerate the retirement of the older generation, something which is not necessarily any more just. This is what a Treasury Board directive issued in May 1985 tried to achieve. By authorising all those who were over 55 to go into early retirement with a generous indemnity, it deprived itself of the most experienced people who had risen through the ranks.

2. The decentralization of the public service would not be an easy task. There is no doubt that the dispersal of decision-making centres would have an adverse effect on efficiency. The transfer of entire families to various parts of the country would be a difficult and gigantic task. Needless to say, it is to be feared that the areas outside the national capital would become a sort of bureaucratic dumping ground.

3. The application of an affirmative action program with quotas to

132

make up for past injustices, at the very moment when resources are lacking, would not be without risk for the beneficiaries.

4. Correcting the distortions in the hierarchy would entail a considerable number of demotions or the application of the Quebec solution which involves shelving, benching or sidelining people whose only shortcoming (in most cases) is tough luck.

5. Increasing salary disparities to take responsiblities into account would likely trigger open war with the union movement and with all Canadians who are not ready to accept that executives at the top of the bureaucracy be paid at the same rates as their counterparts in private enterprise.

6. A policy designed to promote excellence would require recruiting people to pass judgment on the excellence of others, with all the ensuing risks of politicization or of institutionalized mediocrity, not to mention the possibility of politicization and mediocrity emerging simultaneously.

7. Improved communications with the public might be interpreted as propaganda since the services offered by the bureaucracy are monopolistic in nature.

8. A detailed study of life in the public service would stir up such a hornet's nest that even the most carefree minister would be prompted to keep the results safely under lock and key.

9. The idea of a philosophy which takes into account the specific nature of the public service is a theoretical concept necessary for hope but inapplicable, possibly because it is in the nature of the public service to straddle different ethical worlds.

In the concrete world of politics, these nine points have been rolled into a single one on which everything has been focused in a somewhat Procrustean fashion: the size of the public service. The budget tabled on May 23, 1985, announced that the number of federal employees would be cut by 15,000 over five years. Assuming that the public service, if unchecked, would have grown by 15,000 person-years during that time, this amounts to a hypothetical cut of 30,000.

Between theoretical concepts and political action there is a zone of uncertainty from which arise long-term proposals for reshaping a much diminished public service without triggering a blood bath and without forcing large numbers of people to walk the plank. It would be to the advantage of all Canadians to have a closer look at this zone of uncertainty because the public service and all its problems are a microcosm of Canadian society. It is worth recalling that the average age of the Canadian population has started to rise, that the tail end of the baby boom has been sacrificed on the altar of manpower, that federal-provincial confrontations have been the splinters of political life, that women in Canadian society constitute a majority with minority status, that bloating is generalized in management and in services, that pay and taxation systems are sources of conflict and are not coherently matched, and that the school system has created a culture which confuses elitism with racism.

In other words, solutions should not be addressed solely to the public service. Its problems point to the necessity of a new social contract which would be acceptable to all and which would be economically viable.

But let us return to the federal public service and this twilight zone which nobody is interested in precisely because it's so grey. There is a whole range of short-term measures which might be implemented to counteract bloating: a lower retirement age, part-time work with appropriate fringe benefits, leave without pay and retraining programs. These steps would obviously require new provisions for retirement benefits and greater flexibility in working hours. They would free positions and person-years, and at the same time give to part of the population what it wants most of all: time.

The validity of the merit principle could be asserted by re-establishing public service examinations conducted by juries, selected from the public and private sectors as well as from universities, which would establish a universal pool from which government departments would have to choose. Such a system would have the advantage of reducing discrimination. Political personnel would become ineligible for public service appointments before a certain amount of time had elapsed. In the spirit of the Glassco Commission, an independent committee could review public service management, and shield it from political interference. Canadians should reject American practices and place <u>apolitical</u> merit at the top of the values identified with public administration.

At this point arises a thorny problem: who will determine the nature of the federal bureaucracy and the shape it should assume in the coming years? It is not impossible that the political system, supported by a number of pressure groups, will decide to entrust traditionally bureaucratic services to a semi-private sector, outside the public administration proper.

In other words, it may happen that the public service will lose its monopoly on certain functions and become subject to competition from private services.

This would leave us with a federal service whose authority would radiate from the centre towards the periphery by means of the central agencies. The periphery would be made up of a complex network of private consultants, consumers' associations, business representatives, and politicians.

The government side would retain a politically less active role. But it would retain its importance by assuming (perhaps) the role of representing the Canadian mosaic.

But this is a remote hypothesis. In the meantime, the bureaucratic world of Ottawa-Hull must cope with its everyday problems. It must learn to decrease, to age, to avoid running ahead of itself. What remains to be seen is whether it will now contract in the same way as it grew, that is, badly.

NOTES

Introduction

1. Gregory Tardi has raised this question on a number of occasions, as in "The Reach of Government", Policy Options, March 1984.

2. If the 60,000 employees of Canada Post are included in order to compare figures for 1980 with those for 1983, then the Public Service would total 285,000 in the later year.

3. Cf. David K. Foot, Public Employment and Compensation in Canada: Myths and Realities (Montreal: Institute for Research on Public Policy, 1980), p. 188.

4. Auditor General, Annual Report 1976 (Ottawa, Minister of Supply and Services Canada).

5. Quoted by Richard E.B. Simeon, "The Overload Thesis and Canadian Government", Canadian Public Policy, vol. 2, no. 4 (Autumn 1976), p. 542.

6. H.L. Laframboise, "Psychological Distress in the Federal Public Service", unpublished manuscript, May 1979, p. 3. Cf. David Zussman, "The Image of the Public Service in Canada", Canadian Public Administration, vol. 25, no. 1 (Spring 1982), pp. 63-80.

7. Cf. P. Franklin Kilpatrick, Milton C. Cummings, Jr., and Kent M. Jennings, Source Book of a Study of Occupational Values and the Image of the Federal Public Service (Washington, D.C.: Brookings

Institution, 1964); and Stephen Miller, "Bureaucrat Baiting", American Scholar, Spring 1978.

8.   Celebrated expression by Gordon Robertson.

9.   Auditor General, Annual Report 1983 (Ottawa, Minister of Supply and Services Canada), p. 57.

10.   Ibid.

11.   Kenneth Kernaghan, "Canadian Public Administration: Progress and Prospects", in Canadian Public Administration: Discipline and Profession, Kenneth Kernaghan, ed., (Toronto: Butterworth, 1983), p. 5.

12.   Colin Campbell, Governments under Stress (Toronto: University of Toronto Press, 1983), p. 247.

13.   Richard M. Bird and David K. Foot, "Bureaucratic Growth in Canada: Myths and Realities", in The Public Evaluation of Government Spending, G. Bruce Doern and Allan M. Maslove, eds. (Montreal: Institute for Research on Public Policy, 1979), p. 121.

14.   Sandra Gwyn, "Refugees from Ottawa: Five Public Servants and Why They Left", Saturday Night, March 1976, p. 19.

15.   In Ottawa, pre-1865, "there were only about three hundred and fifty civil servants, of all ranks. . . . Professional people and lumber barons were invited to Government House as readily as were the most senior mandarins. . . . Ottawa thus, was a much less self-important place than it is nowadays, much more of a piece with other comparably-sized Canadian communities" (Sandra Gwyn, The Private Capital [Toronto: McClelland and Stewart, 1984], p.41).

Chapter 1

1.   Quoted by J.E. Hodgetts, William McCloskey, Reginal Whitaker and V. Seymour Wilson, The Biography of an Institution, The Civil Service Commission of Canada 1908-1967 (Montreal and Kingston: Institute of Public Administration of Canada, McGill-Queen's University Press, 1972), p. 186.

2.   Many believed that "it is probably a major part of the explanation why the Government went as far as it did to offer special

138

privileges to returned soldiers. They fought off the discontented workers at the same time as they bought off the discontented soldiers" (Ibid., p. 462).

3. See R. MacGregor Dawson, The Civil Service of Canada (London: Oxford University Press, 1929).

4. The first "modern" public service legislation was voted in 1918.

5. J.E. Hodgetts et al., op. cit., p. 463.

6. Many observers believe that the patronage appointments made by Prime Minister Pierre Trudeau in June 1984 caused his successor, John Turner, to lose the federal elections soon afterwards.

7. Nothing better illustrates this point than the cross-examination to which a member of Parliament subjected Henri Bland, Chairman of the powerful Civil Service Commission and responsible for the application of the merit principle in the federal bureaucracy.

    Q. Mr. Chairman, possibly we can get a picture of it in this way: if the total number of marks that could be obtained for a certain position were 100, and the pass mark were 80. . .
    A. Make it 70, it is 70.
    Q. Seventy, and the non-veteran might receive a hundred?
    A. Yes.
    Q. The ordinary veteran might receive 90?
    A. Yes.
    Q. And the disabled veteran might receive 70?
    A. That is a possibility.
    Q. The disabled veteran would get the position?
    A. Yes.
    Quoted by J.E. Hodgetts et al., op. cit., p. 466.

8. Ibid., p. 467. "The single most important piece of legislation was the Veterans Rehabilitation Act. This provided for allowances to be paid any veteran attending vocational training courses, universities, or taking correspondence courses 'likely to fit him for employment or re-employment or to enable him to obtain better or more suitable employment'." Loc. cit.

9. In 1955, 2,800 Newfoundland employees were added to their number.

10. The important social benefits offered permanent employees compensated for salary scales which were quickly outstripped by the cost of living and by wage scales in private enterprise: "Sick

leave, one and one-half day per month, starting with the first month of work but usually not to be drawn on until six months have been completed; special leave of one-half day per month which is to be used for special occasions including death in the family, etc. . . casual leave. . . where you may 'on your honour' take a day or so when you have a bad cold or any other illness that may necessitate only a day or two away from the office without medical attention" (C.J. Sly, "Now You Are a Public Servant", The Public Service Review, June 1950). But these advantages were available solely to permanent employees who represented only one quarter of the public service. The best the other could hope for was that no illness or accident would come and rob them of their job and their place in the sun. In those days, there was no universal medicare plan.

11. Cf. J.E. Hodgetts et al., op. cit. pp. 506-7.

12. In 1946, veterans were offered an education assistance program which, by all accounts, was a great success.

13. "The major reorganization of departments, and especially the creation of a new portfolio was a fairly infrequent event, perhaps occurring every 10 years or so" (Mitchell Sharp, "Decision-making in the Federal Cabinet", Canadian Public Administration, vol. 19, no. 1, [Spring 1976], p. 3).

14. Audrey Doerr, The Machinery of Government in Canada (Toronto: Methuen, 1981), p. 24.

15. "Sir John, so the story goes, suffering from a hangover during his briefing on the British Treasury, grasped the fact that the British had a Treasury Board but went to sleep before he was told the crucial point that the Board had no actual function. Under the mistaken assumption that a Treasury Board was an essential element of British machinery of government, he established the Canadian Treasury Board as a Committee of Cabinet" (Report of the Special Committee on the Review of Personnel Management and the Merit Principle [Ottawa: Minister of Supply and Services Canada, 1979], p. 24).

16. Alexander Mackenzie, Prime Minister from 1873 to 1878, had no secretary and preferred writing by hand.

17. Cf. Mitchell Sharp, op. cit., pp. 3-4.

18. Ibid., p. 3.

19. Ibid. In a similar vein, J.W. Pickersgill used to say that nothing much had changed and that the influence of the mandarins was as strong in 1937 as in 1972.

20. J.L. Granatstein, The Ottawa Men, The Civil Service Mandarins 1935-1957 (Toronto: Oxford University Press, 1982).

21. Christina McCall-Newman, Grits, an Intimate Portrait of the Liberal Party (Toronto: Macmillan of Canada, 1982), p. 220.

22. Kenneth Kernaghan and T.H. McLeod, "Mandarins and Ministers in the Canadian Administrative State", in The Administrative State in Canada, O.P. Dwidedi, ed. (Toronto: University of Toronto Press, 1982), p. 22.

23. J.L. Granatstein, op. cit., p. xi.

24. John Porter, The Vertical Mosaic: An Analysis of Social Class and Power in Canada (Toronto: University of Toronto Press, 1965).

25. J.L. Granatstein, op. cit., p. xi.

26. Ibid., p. 14.

27. Upon taking power, John Diefenbaker promised bloody purges. . . which in fact never took place.

28. Richard A. Easterlin, "What Will 1984 Be Like? Socioeconomic Implications of Recent Twists in Age Structure", Demography, November 1978, pp. 397-432.

29. David Golden, quoted by Douglas Fisher, "Insider's View on How it Got That Way", Executive, February 1982, p. 66.

30. Loc. cit.

31. "Most of the mandarins walked to work each day, or rode the streetcar, talking shop as they travelled. Arnold Heeney, Jack Pickersgill, Louis Rasminsky, and often Lewis Clark, the Chargé d'Affaires at the American Embassy from 1943, regularly hiked into town each day from Rockcliffe. . ." (J.L. Granatstein, op. cit., p. 11).

32. Cf. J.E. Hodgetts et al., op. cit., pp. 236 f.

33. J.E. Hodgetts, The Canadian Public Service: A Physiology of

Government 1867-1970 (Montreal: McGill-Queen's University Press, 1972), p. 160.

34. Cf. W.J. Trudeau, "L'avancement dans le service public", in La Revue du Service civil, Civil Service Federation of Canada, March 1951.

35. Whence the recent success of all books dealing with management and concerned with the idea of excellence.

36. The working week was long: 48 hours, including Saturday morning until 1956. In most offices in Ottawa, employees punched in and out. Since departments did not as a rule have large staffs, it was difficult to cheat. The social ethics of small groups weighed heavily and was particularly efficient in offices where everyone knew each other. Half an hour was allowed for lunch taken at one's desk during the long winter days and which no coffee break interrupted. Only the tea lady broke the monotony of the working day, and occasionally it was possible to treat oneself to a wedge of sugar pie. But the majority of subordinate employees could not afford this kind of luxury on a daily basis.

37. L.W.C.S. Barnes, The Personnel Function in the Federal Public Service (Kingston: Industrial Relations Centre, Queen's University, 1957), p. 16.

38. V. Seymour Wilson, "The Influence of Organizational Theory in Canadian Public Administration", in Canadian Public Administration: Discipline and Profession, Kenneth Kernaghan, ed. (Toronto: Butterworth, 1983), p. 112.

39. H.L. Laframboise, "Administrative Reform in the Federal Public Service: Signs of a Saturation Psychosis", Canadian Public Administration, vol. 14, no. 3 (Fall 1971), p. 308.

40. Ottawa Journal, August 20, 1953.

41. Audrey Doerr, op. cit., p. 2.

42. Civil Service Commission, Annual Report 1955 (Ottawa, Queen's Printer), p. 13.

43. Civil Service Commission, Annual Report 1956 (Ottawa, Queen's Printer), p. 11.

44. Christina McCall-Newman, op. cit., p. 205.

45. Christina Newman, "The Establishment That Governs Us", Saturday Night, May 1968.

46. Rick Van Loon's expression.

47. H.L. Laframboise, "Administrative Reform in the Federal Public Service: Signs of a Saturation Psychosis", op. cit., p. 306.

48. J.E. Hodgetts, op. cit., p. 199.

49. Aaron Wildavsky "A Budget for All Seasons? Why the Traditional Budget Lasts", in The Public Evaluation of Government Spending, G. Bruce Doern and Allan M. Maslove, eds. (Montreal: Institute for Research on Public Policy, 1979), p. 61.

50. R.H. Dowdell quoted by J.E. Hodgetts et al., op. cit., p. 220.

51. Civil Service Commission, Annual Report 1955 (Ottawa, Queen's Printer), p. 10.

Chapter 2

1. A. Doerr, The Machinery of Government in Canada (Toronto: Methuen, 1981), p. 2.

2. W. Clark and Z. Zsigmond, Job Market Reality for Postsecondary Graduates (Ottawa: Statistics Canada, Minister of Supply and Services Canada, 1981), p. 60.

3. See Christopher Lash, The Culture of Narcissism (New York: W.W. Norton, 1978).

4. The idea was developed by V. Seymour Wilson, "The Influence of Organizational Theory in Canadian Public Administration", in Canadian Public Administration: Discipline and Profession, Kenneth Kernaghan, ed. (Toronto: Butterworth, 1983), pp. 103 f.

5. Civil Service Commission, Annual Report 1961 (Ottawa, Queen's Printer), p. 30.

6. Quoted by Richard Gwyn, The Northern Magus (Toronto: McClelland and Stewart, 1980), p. 60.

7. A. Doerr, op. cit., p. 21.

8. M.J.L. Kirby, H.V. Kroeker and W.R. Teschke, "The Impact of Public Policy-Making Structures and Processes in Canada", Canadian Public Administration, vol. 21, no. 3 (Fall 1978), p. 411.

9. Report of the Special Committee on the Review of Personnel

Management and the Merit Principle (Ottawa: Minister of Supply and Services Canada, 1979), p. 67.

10. L.W.C.S. Barnes, The Personnel Function in the Federal Public Service (Kingston: Industrial Relations Centre, Queen's University, 1957), p. 3.

11. "Slash" is the appropriate word, the report being unusually harsh.

12. A. Doerr, op. cit., pp. 52-53.

13. Interim Report on Relations Between the Government of Canada and the Province of Quebec: 1967-1977, 1977, Federal-Provincial Relations Office, p. 12.

14. J.L. Granatstein, The Ottawa Men, The Civil Service Mandarins 1935-1957 (Toronto: Oxford University Press, 1982), p. 5.

15. The Commission "launched a massive language training program for civil servants, which, given sufficient time, should enable it to administer realistically the complex and rather drastic requirements now spelled out in the Act" (J.E. Hodgetts, The Canadian Public Service, A Physiology of Government 1867-1970 [Montreal: McGill-Queen's University Press, 1972], p. 38).

16. "The preparatory Committee on Collective Bargaining which reported in 1965 found, to no one's particular surprise, that the 138,000 continuing positions then under the Civil Service Act were allocated to 700 classes and to about 1,700 grades within those classes. The 24,000 men and women who came under the provisions of the Prevailing Rate Employees General Regulations had 1,250 job titles between them and even the 3,000 employees who were covered by the Ships Officers and Crews Regulations were known by 130 different job titles" (L.W.C.S. Barnes, op. cit., p. 7).

Chapter 3

1. Anthony King, "Overload, Problems of Governing in the 1970s", Political Studies, vol. 27 (June-September 1975), p. 286.

2. M.J.L. Kirby, H.V. Kroeker and W.R. Teschke, "The Impact of Public Policy-Making Structures and Processes in Canada", Canadian Public Administration vol. 21, no. 3 (Fall 1978), p. 411.

3. See Richard D. French, <u>How Ottawa Decides, Planning and Industrial Policy-Making 1968-1980</u> (Toronto: James Lorimer & Company, in association with the Canadian Institute for Economic Policy, 1980), pp. 18 f.

4. Canadians are unaware of the incredible prestige enjoyed by the federal bureaucracy during the 1970s. I heard it praised on several occasions in Paris, where people are past masters at systematically criticizing everyone and everything.

5. Quoted by George Radwanski, <u>Trudeau</u> (Toronto: Macmillan of Canada, 1978), p. 149.

6. Richard D. French, op. cit., p. 21.

7. Richard Gwyn, <u>The Northern Magus</u> (Toronto: McClelland and Stewart, 1980), p. 93.

8. "His enemies, including Cabinet Ministers, call him 'a big black spider'. Almost alone among the key mandarins, Pitfield has never been invited to join the Five Lakes Fishing Club, the retreat in the Gatineau Hills where deputy ministers gather off duty to fish, canoe, hike and trade gossip" (Richard Gwyn, op. cit., p. 76).

9. H.L. Laframboise, "Counter-Managers: The Abandonment of Unity of Command", <u>Optimum</u>, vol. 8, no. 4 (1977), pp. 18-28.

10. I write "men" because according to all evidence women were never included in the grandiose plans of the Prime Minister's Office.

11. <u>Notes for Remarks by the Prime Minister at the Harrison Liberal Conference</u> (Typescript, Harrison Hot Springs, B.C., November 21, 1969).

12. Richard D. French, op. cit., p. 22.

13. H.L. Laframboise, "The Future of the Public Administration in Canada", <u>Canadian Public Administration</u>, vol. 25, no. 4 (Winter 1982), p. 507.

14. M.J.L. Kirby and H.V. Kroeker, "The Politics of Crisis Management in Government: Does Planning Make Any Difference?" in <u>Studies on Crisis Management</u>, C.F. Smart and

W.T. Stanbury, eds. (Montreal: Institute for Research on Public Policy/Butterworth, 1978), p. 185.

15. Quoted by Stephen Duncan, "Emasculated Mandarins", Financial Post, January 25, 1975.

16. Colin Campbell and George J. Szablowski, The Superbureaucrats, Structure and Behaviour in Central Agencies (Toronto: Macmillan of Canada, 1979).

17. John Porter, The Vertical Mosaic: An Analysis of Social Class and Power in Canada (Toronto: University of Toronto Press, 1965).

18. Cf. Colin Campbell and George J. Szablowski, op. cit., pp. 113-14.

19. Ibid., p. 129.

20. P.J. Chartrand and K.K. Pond, A Study of Executive Career Paths in the Public Service of Canada (Chicago: Public Personnel Association, 1970).

21. Colin Campbell and George J. Szablowski, op. cit., p. 116.

22. Cf. Richard Gwyn, op. cit., p. 98.

23. Colin Campbell and George J. Szablowski, op. cit., p. 127.

24. Ibid., p. 137.

25. D.G. Hartle, interviewed by Sandra Gwyn, "Refugees from Ottawa: Five Public Servants and Why They Left", Saturday Night, March 1976.

26. Audrey Doerr, The Machinery of Government in Canada (Toronto: Methuen, 1981), p. 108.

27. H.L. Laframboise, "Here Come the Program-Benders", Optimum, vol. 7, no. 1 (1976), p. 41.

28. Roch Bolduc, "Les cadres supérieurs, quinze ans après", Administration publique canadienne, vol. 21, no. 4 (Winter 1978), p. 264.

29. Report of the Royal Commission on Financial Management and Accountability (Ottawa: Minister of Supply and Services Canada, 1979), pp. 193-94.

30. D.G. Hartle, "Techniques and Processes of Administration", Canadian Public Administration, vol. 19, no. 1 (Spring 1976), p. 27.

31. See Interim Report on Relations Between the Government of Canada and the Province of Quebec 1967-1977, Federal-Provincial Relations Office, 1977.

32. D.G. Hartle, quoted by Sandra Gwyn, op. cit.

33. Audrey Doerr, op. cit., p. 5.

34. Quoted by Sandra Gwyn, op. cit.

Chapter 4

1. "Professor Henry Mintzberg of McGill caused a stir in the business community by observing that the textbook version of how managers operate is a fantasy. Managers may pay lip service to planning and tables of organization, pointed out Mintzberg, but they actually function quite well in near chaos. In a subsequent article, he identified managers as holistic, intuitive thinkers who 'revel in ambiguity, in complex mysterious systems with relatively little order'" (H.L. Laframboise, "Counter-Managers: The Abandonment of the Unity of Command", Optimum, vol. 8, no. 4 [1977], p. 25).

2. Audrey Doerr, The Machinery of Government in Canada (Toronto: Methuen, 1981), p. 6.

3. Mitchell Sharp, "The Role of the Mandarins", Policy Options, May-June 1981.

4. Audrey Doerr, op. cit., pp. 25-26.

5. Richard Gwyn, The Northern Magus (Toronto: McClelland and Stewart, 1980), p. 312.

6. Peter Foster, The Sorcerer's Apprentices, Canada's Superbureaucrats and the Energy Mess (Toronto: Collins, 1982), p. 47.

7. See Audrey Doerr, op. cit., p. 56.

8. A. Campbell, Governments Under Stress, Political Executives and Key Bureaucrats in Washington, London, and Ottawa (Toronto: University of Toronto Press, 1983), p. 199.

9. D.G. Hartle, "Techniques and Processes of Administration", Canadian Public Administration, vol. 19, no. 1 (Spring 1976), p. 30.

10. Paul Pross, "From System to Serendipity: The Practise and Study of Public Policy in the Trudeau Years", in Canadian Public Administration: Discipline and Profession, Kenneth Kernaghan, ed. (Toronto: Butterworth, 1983), p. 90.

11. D.G. Hartle, The Draft Memorandum to Cabinet (Toronto: Institute of Public Administration of Canada, 1977).

12. Benefits and Perquisites Attitudes Survey (Ottawa: Treasury Board of Canada, March 1982), p. 18.

13. D. Fowke, "Towards a Theory of Public Administration for Canada", Canadian Public Administration, vol. 19, no. 1 (Spring 1976), p. 35.

14. Hugh Heclo and Aaron Wildavsky, The Private Government of Public Money: Community and Policy Inside British Politics (Berkeley: University of California Press, 1974), p. LXVI.

15. Auditor General, Annual Report 1983 (Ottawa, Minister of Supply and Services Canada), p. 63.

16. Jeffrey L. Pressman and Aaron Wildavsky, Implementation (Berkeley: University of California Press, 1973).

17. Quoted by Colin Campbell, op. cit., p. 82.

18. Report of the Special Committee on the Review of Personnel Management and the Merit Principle (Ottawa: Minister of Supply and Services Canada, 1979), pp. 48-49.

Chapter 5

1. "Rarely, if ever, does it make strategic sense for a department to reveal its aspirations during the regular cyclical budgetary review. Better to introduce initiatives by means of special requests to Cabinet outside the regular budgetary cycle when the competition for funds is less. . ." (D.G. Hartle, "Techniques and Processes of Administration", Canadian Public Administration, vol. 19, no. 1 [Spring 1976], p. 25).

2. Cf. The Financial Post, August 16, 1975.

3. Jim Steinhart, "Slash the Public Service, It Is Easier Said Than Done", Executive, vol. 24., no. 1 (January 1982), p. 44.

THE MEMBERS OF THE INSTITUTE

Board of Directors
The Honourable John B. Aird, O.C., Q.C.
  (Honorary Chairman)
  Aird & Berlis, Toronto
The Honourable Robert L. Stanfield,
  P.C., Q.C., (Chairman), Ottawa
Claudine Sotiau (Vice-Chairman)
  Ducros, Meilleur, Roy et associés ltée
  Montréal
Roger Charbonneau
  Président du conseil d'administration
  Banque Nationale de Paris (Canada)
  Montréal
Louis A. Desrochers, Q.C.
  McCuaig, Desrochers, Edmonton
Dr. Rod Dobell
  President, The Institute for Research
  on Public Policy, Victoria
Dr. Henry E. Duckworth, O.C.
  President Emeritus
  University of Winnipeg
Dr. Regis Duffy
  President
  Diagnostic Chemicals Ltd.
  Charlottetown
Dr. James D. Fleck
  Faculty of Management Studies
  University of Toronto
Peter C. Godsoe
  Vice Chairman of the Board
  The Bank of Nova Scotia, Toronto
Dianne I. Hall
  Senior Vice-President,
  NOVA, AN ALBERTA
  CORPORATION, Calgary
Grace Hartman
  President Emeritus, CUPE
  Willowdale
David Hennigar
  Atlantic Regional Director
  Burns Fry Limited, Halifax

Roland J. Lutes, C.A.
  Clarkson Gordon, Montreal
Dr. Patrick O'Flaherty
  Head, Department of English
  Language and Literature, Memorial
  University of Newfoundland, St. John's
Dr. Tom Pepper
  Pepper Consultants Ltd., Saskatoon
Guy Roberge, C.R.,
  Conseil
  Clarkson, Tétrault, Ottawa
Thérèse P. Sévigny
  Vice-présidente à la communication
  Société Radio-Canada, Ottawa

President
Rod Dobell

Secretary
Peter C. Dobell
  Director, Parliamentary Centre
  for Foreign Affairs and Foreign
  Trade, Ottawa

Treasurer
Parker Staples
  Director, Financial Services
  The Institute for Research on
  Public Policy, Halifax

Executive Committee
The Honourable Robert L. Stanfield
  (Chairman)
Claudine Sotiau (Vice-Chairman)
Peter C. Dobell
Rod Dobell
Roland J. Lutes
Parker Staples

Investment Committee
Marcel Cazavan
Peter C. Dobell
Peter C. Godsoe
Michael Koerner

149

Council of Trustees
Members at Large
Dr. Stefan Dupré (Chairman)
Department of Political Science
University of Toronto
Doris H. Anderson, O.C.
Toronto
Professor Kell Antoft
Institute of Public Affairs
Dalhousie University, Halifax
Marie-Andrée Bertrand
École de criminologie
Université de Montréal
Dr. Roger A. Blais
École Polytechnique de Montréal
George Cooper, Q.C.
McInnes, Cooper and Robertson
Halifax
James S. Cowan, Q.C.
Partner, Stewart, MacKeen &
Covert, Halifax
V. Edward Daughney
President, First City Trust
Company, Vancouver
Dr. Wendy Dobson
Executive Director
C.D. Howe Institute, Toronto
Marc Eliesen
Chairperson
Manitoba Energy Authority
Winnipeg
Emery Fanjoy
Secretary, Council of Maritime
Premiers, Halifax
Dr. Allan K. Gillmore
Executive Director, Association of
Universities and Colleges of
Canada, Ottawa
Dr. Donald Glendenning
President, Holland College
Charlottetown
Margaret C. Harris
Past President, The National
Council of Women of Canada
Saskatoon
Richard W. Johnston
President, Spencer Stuart &
Associates, Toronto
Dr. Leon Katz, O.C.
Saskatoon
Terrence Mactaggart
Managing Director
Sound Linked Data Inc.
Mississauga

Dr. John S. McCallum
Faculty of Administrative Studies
University of Manitoba, Winnipeg
Claude Morin
École nationale d'administration
publique, Québec
Milan Nastich
Canadian General Investments
Limited, Toronto
Professor William A. W. Neilson
Dean, Faculty of Law
University of Victoria
Roderick C. Nolan, P.Eng.
Executive Vice-President
Neill & Gunter Limited, Fredericton
Robert J. Olivero
United Nations Secretariat
New York
Maureen O'Neil
Co-ordinator Status of Women Canada,
Ottawa
Garnet T. Page, O.C.
Calgary
Dr. Gilles Paquet
Dean, Faculty of Administration
University of Ottawa
Dr. K. George Pedersen
President, University of Western
Ontario, London
Professor Marilyn L. Pilkington
Osgoode Hall Law School, Toronto
Dr. David W. Slater
Ottawa
Dr. Stuart L. Smith
Chairman Science Council of
Canada, Ottawa
Eldon D. Thompson
President, Telesat, Vanier
Marc-Adélard Tremblay, O.C.
Departement d'anthropologie
Université Laval, Québec
Dr. Israel Unger
Department of Chemistry University of
New Brunswick, Fredericton
Philip Vineberg, O.C., Q.C.
Phillips & Vineberg, Montreal
Dr. Norman Wagner
President, University of Calgary
Ida Wasacase, C.M.
Winnipeg
Dr. R. Sherman Weaver
Director, Alberta Environmental
Centre, Vegreville

150

Dr. Blossom Wigdor
  Director, Program in Gerontology
  University of Toronto

Government Representatives
Herb Clarke, Newfoundland
Joseph H. Clarke, Nova Scotia
Michael Decter, Manitoba
Jim Dinning, Alberta
Hershell Ezrin, Ontario
Honourable Lowell Murray, Canada
John H. Parker, Northwest Territories
Henry Phillips, Prince Edward Island
Norman Riddell, Saskatchewan
Jean-K. Samson, Québec
Norman Spector, British Columbia
Eloise Spitzer, Yukon
Barry Toole, New Brunswick

INSTITUTE MANAGEMENT

Rod Dobell   President
Louis Vagianos   Special Assistant

Edgar Gallant   Fellow-in-Residence
Tom Kent   Fellow-in-Residence
Eric Kierans   Fellow-in-Residence
Jean-Luc Pepin   Fellow-in-Residence
Gordon Robertson   Fellow-in-Residence

Yvon Gasse   Director, Small and Medium-Sized Business Program
Barbara L. Hodgins   Director, Western Resources Program
Barry Lesser   Director, Regional Employment Opportunities Program
Frank Stone   A/Director, International Economics Program

Shirley Seward   Director, Co-ordination and Liaison
Parker Staples   Director, Financial Services & Treasurer
Donald Wilson   Director, Communications

Tom Kent   Editor, *Policy Options Politiques*

PUBLICATIONS AVAILABLE - APRIL 1986

Order Address:	The Institute for Research on Public Policy P.O. Box 3670 South Halifax, Nova Scotia B3J 3K6
Leroy O. Stone & Claude Marceau	*Canadian Population Trends and Public Policy Through the 1980s.* 1977 $4.00
Raymond Breton	*The Canadian Condition: A Guide to Research in Public Policy.* 1977 $2.95
Raymond Breton	*Une orientation de la recherche politique dans le contexte canadien.* 1977 $2.95
J.W. Rowley & W.T. Stanbury (eds.)	*Competition Policy in Canada: Stage II, Bill C-13.* 1978 $12.95
C.F. Smart & W.T. Stanbury (eds.)	*Studies on Crisis Management.* 1978 $9.95
W.T. Stanbury (ed.)	*Studies on Regulation in Canada.* 1978 $9.95
Michael Hudson	*Canada in the New Monetary Order: Borrow? Devalue? Restructure!* 1978 $6.95
David K. Foot (ed.)	*Public Employment and Compensation in Canada: Myths and Realities.* 1978 $10.95
Raymond Breton & Gail Grant Akian	*Urban Institutions and People of Indian Ancestry: Suggestions for Research.* 1979 $3.00
Thomas H. Atkinson	*Trends in Life Satisfaction Among Canadians, 1968-1977.* 1979 $3.00
W.E. Cundiff & Mado Reid (eds.)	*Issues in Canadian/U.S. Transborder Computer Data Flows.* 1979 $6.50
Meyer W. Bucovetsky (ed.)	*Studies in Public Employment and Compensation in Canada.* 1979 $14.95
Richard French & André Béliveau	*The RCMP and the Management of National Security.* 1979 $6.95
Richard French & André Béliveau	*La GRC et la gestion de la sécurité nationale.* 1979 $6.95

G. Bruce Doern & Allan M. Maslove (eds.)	*The Public Evaluation of Government Spending.* 1979 $10.95
Leroy O. Stone & Michael J. MacLean	*Future Income Prospects for Canada's Senior Citizens.* 1979 $7.95
Richard M. Bird	*The Growth of Public Employment in Canada.* 1979 $12.95
Richard J. Schultz	*Federalism and the Regulatory Process.* 1979 $1.50
Richard J. Schultz	*Le fédéralisme et le processus de réglementation.* 1979 $1.50
Lionel D. Feldman & Katherine A. Graham	*Bargaining for Cities, Municipalities and Intergovernmental Relations: An Assessment.* 1979 $10.95
Elliot J. Feldman & Neil Nevitte (eds.)	*The Future of North America: Canada, the United States, and Quebec Nationalism.* 1979 $7.95
David R. Protheroe	*Imports and Politics: Trade Decision Making in Canada, 1968-1979.* 1980 $8.95
G. Bruce Doern	*Government Intervention in the Canadian Nuclear Industry.* 1980 $8.95
G. Bruce Doern & Robert W. Morrison (eds.)	*Canadian Nuclear Policies.* 1980 $14.95
Allan M. Maslove & Gene Swimmer	*Wage Controls in Canada: 1975-78: A Study of Public Decision Making.* 1980 $11.95
T. Gregory Kane	*Consumers and the Regulators: Intervention in the Federal Regulatory Process.* 1980 $10.95
Réjean Lachapelle & Jacques Henripin	*La situation démolinguistique au Canada: évolution passée et prospective.* 1980 $24.95
Albert Breton & Anthony Scott	*The Design of Federations.* 1980 $6.95
A.R. Bailey & D.G. Hull	*The Way Out: A More Revenue-Dependent Public Sector and How It Might Revitalize the Process of Governing.* 1980 $6.95
David R. Harvey	*Christmas Turkey or Prairie Vulture? An Economic Analysis of the Crow's Nest Pass Grain Rates.* 1980 $10.95
Donald G. Cartwright	*Official Language Populations in Canada: Patterns and Contacts.* 1980 $4.95
Richard M. Bird	*Taxing Corporations.* 1980 $6.95
Leroy O. Stone & Susan Fletcher	*A Profile of Canada's Older Population.* 1980 $7.95
Peter N. Nemetz (ed.)	*Resource Policy: International Perspectives.* 1980 $18.95

Keith A.J. Hay (ed.)	*Canadian Perspectives on Economic Relations With Japan.* 1980 $18.95
Dhiru Patel	*Dealing With Interracial Conflict: Policy Alternatives.* 1980 $5.95
Raymond Breton & Gail Grant	*La langue de travail au Québec : synthèse de la recherche sur la rencontre de deux langues.* 1981 $10.95
Diane Vanasse	*L'évolution de la population scolaire du Québec.* 1981 $12.95
David M. Cameron (ed.)	*Regionalism and Supranationalism: Challenges and Alternatives to the Nation-State in Canada and Europe.* 1981 $9.95
Heather Menzies	*Women and the Chip: Case Studies of the Effects of Information on Employment in Canada.* 1981 $8.95
H.V. Kroeker (ed.)	*Sovereign People or Sovereign Governments.* 1981 $12.95
Peter Aucoin (ed.)	*The Politics and Management of Restraint in Government.* 1981 $17.95
Nicole S. Morgan	*Nowhere to Go? Possible Consequences of the Demographic Imbalance in Decision-Making Groups of the Federal Public Service.* 1981 $8.95
Nicole S. Morgan	*Où aller? Les conséquences prévisibles des déséquilibres démographiques chez les groupes de décision de la fonction publique fédérale.* 1981 $8.95
Raymond Breton, Jeffrey G. Reitz & Victor F. Valentine	*Les frontières culturelles et la cohésion du Canada.* 1981 $18.95
Peter N. Nemetz (ed.)	*Energy Crisis: Policy Response.* 1981 $10.95
James Gillies	*Where Business Fails.* 1981 $9.95
Allan Tupper & G. Bruce Doern (eds.)	*Public Corporations and Public Policy in Canada.* 1981 $16.95
Réjean Lachapelle & Jacques Henripin	*The Demolinguistic Situation in Canada: Past Trends and Future Prospects.* 1982 $24.95
Irving Brecher	*Canada's Competition Policy Revisited: Some New Thoughts on an Old Story.* 1982 $3.00
Ian McAllister	*Regional Development and the European Community: A Canadian Perspective.* 1982 $13.95
Donald J. Daly	*Canada in an Uncertain World Economic Environment.* 1982 $3.00
W.T. Stanbury & Fred Thompson	*Regulatory Reform in Canada.* 1982 $7.95

157

Robert J. Buchan, C. Christopher Johnston, T. Gregory Kane, Barry Lesser, Richard J. Schultz & W.T. Stanbury	*Telecommunications Regulation and the Constitution.* 1982 $18.95
Rodney de C. Grey	*United States Trade Policy Legislation: A Canadian View.* 1982 $7.95
John Quinn & Philip Slayton (eds.)	*Non-Tariff Barriers After the Tokyo Round.* 1982 $17.95
Stanley M. Beck & Ivan Bernier (eds.)	*Canada and the New Constitution: The Unfinished Agenda.* 2 vols. 1983 $10.95 (set)
R. Brian Woodrow & Kenneth B. Woodside (eds.)	*The Introduction of Pay-TV in Canada: Issues and Implications.* 1983 $14.95
E.P. Weeks & L. Mazany	*The Future of the Atlantic Fisheries.* 1983 $5.00
Douglas D. Purvis (ed.), assisted by Frances Chambers	*The Canadian Balance of Payments: Perspectives and Policy Issues.* 1983 $24.95
Roy A. Matthews	*Canada and the "Little Dragons": An Analysis of Economic Developments in Hong Kong, Taiwan, and South Korea and the Challenge/ Opportunity They Present for Canadian Interests in the 1980s.* 1983 $11.95
Charles Pearson & Gerry Salembier	*Trade, Employment, and Adjustment.* 1983 $5.00
Steven Globerman	*Cultural Regulation in Canada.* 1983 $11.95
F.R. Flatters & R.G. Lipsey	*Common Ground for the Canadian Common Market.* 1983 $5.00
Frank Bunn, assisted by U. Domb, D. Huntley, H. Mills, H. Silverstein	*Oceans from Space: Towards the Management of Our Coastal Zones.* 1983 $5.00
C.D. Shearing & P.C. Stenning	*Private Security and Private Justice: The Challenge of the 80s.* 1983 $5.00
Jacob Finkelman & Shirley B. Goldenberg	*Collective Bargaining in the Public Service: The Federal Experience in Canada.* 2 vols. 1983 $29.95 (set)
Gail Grant	*The Concrete Reserve: Corporate Programs for Indians in the Urban Work Place.* 1983 $5.00
Owen Adams & Russell Wilkins	*Healthfulness of Life.* 1983 $8.00
Yoshi Tsurumi with Rebecca R. Tsurumi	*Sogoshosha: Engines of Export-Based Growth.* (Revised Edition). 1984 $10.95
Raymond Breton & Gail Grant (eds.)	*The Dynamics of Government Programs for Urban Indians in the Prairie Provinces.* 1984 $19.95

Frank Stone

Canada, The GATT and the International Trade System. 1984 $15.00

Pierre Sauvé

Private Bank Lending and Developing-Country Debt. 1984 $10.00

Mark Thompson & Gene Swimmer

Conflict or Compromise: The Future of Public Sector Industrial Relations. 1984 $15.00

Samuel Wex

Instead of FIRA: Autonomy for Canadian Subsidiaries? 1984 $8.00

R.J. Wonnacott

Selected New Developments in International Trade Theory. 1984 $7.00

R.J. Wonnacott

Aggressive US Reciprocity Evaluated with a New Analytical Approach to Trade Conflicts. 1984 $8.00

Richard W. Wright

Japanese Business in Canada: The Elusive Alliance. 1984 $12.00

Paul K. Gorecki & W.T. Stanbury

The Objectives of Canadian Competition Policy, 1888-1983. 1984 $15.00

Michael Hart

Some Thoughts on Canada-United States Sectoral Free Trade. 1985 $7.00

J. Peter Meekison Roy J. Romanow & William D. Moull

Origins and Meaning of Section 92A: The 1982 Constitutional Amendment on Resources. 1985 $10.00

Conference Papers

Canada and International Trade. Volume One: Major Issues of Canadian Trade Policy. Volume Two: Canada and the Pacific Rim. 1985 $25.00 (set)

A.E. Safarian

Foreign Direct Investment: A Survey of Canadian Research. 1985 $8.00

Joseph R. D'Cruz & James D. Fleck

Canada Can Compete! Strategic Management of the Canadian Industrial Portfolio. 1985 $18.00

Barry Lesser & Louis Vagianos

Computer Communications and the Mass Market in Canada. 1985 $10.00

W.R. Hines

Trade Policy Making in Canada: Are We Doing it Right? 1985 $10.00

Bertrand Nadeau

Britain's Entry into the European Economic Community and its Effect on Canada's Agricultural Exports. 1985 $10.00

Paul B. Huber

Promoting Timber Cropping: Policies Toward Non-Industrial Forest Owners in New Brunswick. 1985 $10.00

Gordon Robertson

Northern Provinces: A Mistaken Goal. 1985 $8.00

159

Petr Hanel

La technologie et les exportations canadiennes du matériel pour la filière bois-papier. 1985 $20.00

Russel M. Wills,
Steven Globerman &
Peter J. Booth

Software Policies for Growth and Export. 1986 $15.00

Marc Malone

Une place pour le Québec au Canada. 1986 $20.00

A. R. Dobell &
S. H. Mansbridge

The Social Policy Process in Canada. 1986 $8.00

William D. Shipman (ed.)

Trade and Investment Across the Northeast Boundary: Quebec, the Atlantic Provinces, and New England. 1986 $20.00

Nicole Morgan

Implosion: An Analysis of the Growth of the Federal Public Service in Canada (1945-1985). 1986 $20.00

Nicole Morgan

Implosion: analyse de la croissance de la Fonction publique fédérale canadienne (1945-1985). 1986 $20.00

Printed in Canada